BLACKLISTED!

ISTED!

AND THE FIRST AMENDMENT

CALKINS CREEK
AN IMPRINT OF HIGHLIGHTS

Title page photo: Members of the Hollywood Ten surrounded by their families and supporters.

"If a man is a Communist and denies his affiliation before the committee, he has committed perjury and will go to jail. If he answers affirmatively, the second question put to him will be 'Who else?'"

For information about permission to reproduce selections from this book,
please contact permissions@highlights.com.

Calkins Creek
An Imprint of Highlights
815 Church Street
Honesdale, Pennsylvania 18431
calkinscreekbooks.com
Printed in China

ISBN: 978-1-62091-603-2 (hardcover)
ISBN: 978-1-68437-144-0 (eBook)
Library of Congress Control Number: 2018931176

First edition
10 9 8 7 6 5 4 3 2 1

Design by Barbara Grzeslo
The text is set in Sabon.
The titles are set in Impact.

For all who cherish the Constitution of the United States and the freedoms it guarantees.

—LDB

CONTENTS

"It is a very dangerous precedent when a government body without any judicial function assumes one and still claims it is not subject to any rules of judicial procedure."

—Gordon Kahn

AMERICA FIGHTS

Although Russia had been America's ally against Nazi Germany in World War II, a communist scare—sometimes called the Red Scare or Red Menace based on the main color of the Soviet Union's flag—swept the United States immediately following the war. Russia's influence in the world was expanding, and communist governments were springing up in countries around the globe. In communism as it was practiced in the Soviet Union in 1947, the government owned all industries and property as part of its attempt to create a society where everyone was equal; private ownership of property was forbidden. Some people in the United States worried

THE RED SCARE

that communists had infiltrated key positions in government and businesses in order to sway public thinking against America's system of free enterprise, where private businesses compete mostly without the interference of the government. The House of Representatives gave its Committee on Un-American Activities (HUAC) the task of looking into whether communists had infiltrated American society, and where. The HUAC's investigations and hearings were supposed to lead to new laws to combat this communist threat.

THE PLAYERS

THE COMMITTEE

J. PARNELL THOMAS, Republican, New Jersey; Chairman • **KARL E. MUNDT**, Republican, South Dakota • **JOHN MCDOWELL**, Republican, Pennsylvania • **RICHARD M. NIXON**, Republican, California • **RICHARD B. VAIL**, Republican, Illinois • **JOHN S. WOOD**, Democrat, Georgia • **JOHN E. RANKIN**, Democrat, Mississippi • **J. HARDIN PETERSON**, Democrat, Florida • **HERBERT C. BONNER**, Democrat, North Carolina • **ROBERT E. STRIPLING**, Chief Investigator and Permanent Seccretary

THE NINETEEN SUBPOENAED WITNESSES

ALVAH BESSIE, screenwriter* • **HERBERT BIBERMAN**, screenwriter* • **BERTOLT BRECHT**, playwright, director • **LESTER COLE**, screenwriter* • **RICHARD COLLINS**, screenwriter • **EDWARD DMYTRYK**, director* • **GORDON KAHN**, screenwriter • **HOWARD KOCH**, screenwriter • **RING LARDNER JR.**, screenwriter* • **JOHN HOWARD LAWSON**, screenwriter* • **ALBERT MALTZ**, screenwriter* • **LEWIS MILESTONE**, director • **SAMUEL ORNITZ**, screenwriter* • **LARRY PARKS**, actor • **IRVING PICHEL**, director • **ROBERT ROSSEN**, director • **WALDO SALT**, screenwriter • **ADRIAN SCOTT**, producer* • **DALTON TRUMBO**, screenwriter*

denotes one of the Hollywood Ten

ATTORNEYS FOR THE NINETEEN

BARTLEY C. CRUM • **CHARLES J. KATZ** • **ROBERT W. KENNY** • **BEN MARGOLIS** • **MARTIN POPPER** • **SAMUEL ROSENWEIN**

SUMMONED
TO WASHINGTON

On October 20, 1947, the city of Washington was tense as the House of Representatives' Committee on Un-American Activities (HUAC) prepared to begin its "investigation into alleged subversive influence in America's motion-picture industry." Screenwriter Gordon Kahn, an eyewitness to the HUAC hearings, described the atmosphere in the District of Columbia as "like that on the eve of a coronation—or an important hanging." By nine o'clock that fall morning, a long line of spectators crowded into the rotunda on the second floor of the Cannon House Office Building. They were waiting to be admitted to the Caucus Room, where the hearings would be held, and perhaps to catch sight of a Hollywood celebrity.

SUBVERSION

"The act of subverting: the state of being subverted; *especially*: a systematic attempt to overthrow or undermine a government or political system by persons working secretly from within."

J. Parnell Thomas, the chairman of the committee, already had worked with newsreel cameramen over the weekend to prepare the Caucus Room for the big event. A battery of five cameras flanked one side of the great hall. Powerful lights illuminated the raised stage where the committee would be sitting, and overhead, high-intensity bulbs replaced those usually used in the four ornate crystal chandeliers that hung from the ceiling. "Four majors [*sic*] radio networks" would be on hand to cover the hearings, which were estimated to last three weeks. "Press arrangements [had] been made for 125 [reporters]. Despite . . . being Washington's largest hearing room, space for the public [would] be SRO [standing-room only]."

On the Saturday before the hearings began, Thomas had even made a practice run. On cue, he strode out from a doorway at the rear of the stage and took his seat. Unfortunately, the representative was short in stature. According to Kahn, when Thomas sat, he disappeared from camera view. A cameraman slipped a District of Columbia telephone directory and red silk pillow onto the chair, and the representative reseated himself. With the added elevation, Thomas was ready for his close-up.

The room looked like a Hollywood movie set. In every sense, that is what it was. The HUAC hearings were not only being held to determine how deeply communists had infiltrated the Hollywood film community, but they were also for show. Communism wasn't illegal in the United States, nor was belonging to the Communist Party USA a crime. But communism was the political system of the Union of Soviet Socialist Republics (USSR, sometimes called the Soviet Union or Russia), America's main Cold War enemy immediately after World War II. The committee members wanted to intimidate American communists, while also demonstrating to their constituents that they were working to keep the country safe from Russia's form of government. It was never too early to begin preparing for the next election.

Oddly, nowhere in that great room was there an American flag, a symbol of the United States and one of its basic principles: to think freely according to one's own beliefs.

Across town at the Shoreham Hotel, less than ten miles from the U.S. Capitol and the Cannon House Office Building, nineteen men—"twelve screenwriters, five directors, a producer, and an actor"—and their attorneys had spent Sunday evening preparing their statements and strategy. They had been summoned to Washington, DC, to testify before the HUAC. The subpoenas ordering them to appear had come as no surprise to any of the men. Thomas had released a statement to the press on September 21 naming those he was calling to Washington. Even so, being served a subpoena by a U.S. marshal was frightening. Years later, Lester Cole, one of the nineteen, recalled his family's feelings upon receiving his summons: "The fear, chaos, and uncertainty are not easy to describe. The reaction among the families of others subpoenaed could not have been much different from that of mine. Jonnie [Cole's wife] was shocked and fearful. The radio reports frightened [his sons] Michael and Jeffry [sic]. I tried desperately to make light of it . . . to reassure them it was all newspaper talk, but . . . my voice could not help but betray my own deep concern."

By the time Thomas pounded his gavel at 10:30 that Monday morning to bring the HUAC hearings to order, the people who had been waiting outside the Caucus Room were seated. Newsreel cameras whirred. Photographers' flashbulbs popped. To the press, the chairman had already promised to unveil "several surprises"

21

September 19, 1947

Honorable J. Parnell Thomas, Chairman of the Committee on Un-American Activities issued the following statement for release Sunday morning newspapers, September 21, 1947:

"Subpoenaes have been issued and are now in the process of being served upon the following witnesses to appear in Washington beginning October 20 in connection with the Committee on Un-American Activities' forthcoming hearing on communist influences in the motion picture industry:

Alva H. Bessie	James McGuiness
Roy E. Brewer	Lewis Milestone
Herbert Biberman	Adolph Menjou
Berthold Brecht	Sam Moore
Lester Cole	John Charles Moffitt
Gary Cooper	Robert Montgomery
Charles Chaplin	George Murphy
Joseph E. Davies	Clifford Odets
Walt Disney	Larry Parks
Edward Dmytryk	William Pomerance
Cedric Gibbons	Ronald Reagan
Samuel Goldwyn	Lela E. Rogers
Rupert Hughes	Howard Rushmore
Eric Johnston	Morrie Ryskind
Howard Koch	Adrian Scott
Ring Lardner, Jr.	Dore Schary
John Howard Lawson	Donald Ogden Stewart
Louis B. Mayer	Robert Taylor
Albert Maltz	Waldo Salt
Thomas Leo McCarey	Dalton Trumbo
Lowell Mellett	Jack L. Warner
	Sam Wood

The order of appearance of the witnesses will be announced at a later date.

In making public the names of the witnesses, however, I want to emphasize that the mere fact they are being called to testify before the Committee should not be considered a reflection in any way upon their character or patriotism. These persons are being brought with the sole objective of obtaining the facts regarding the inroads the communists have made in Hollywood. Some of the witnesses are friendly to the Committee's purposes. Others are undoubtedly hostile. The Committee wants to hear both sides.

over the course of the hearings.

"The committee," Thomas began, "is well aware of the magnitude of the subject which it is investigating." It feared that movies—with an audience that stretched from coast to coast, in cities, suburbs, and rural areas—were an ideal way to spread the communist message, to broadcast communist propaganda. Thomas explained, "With such vast influence over the lives of American citizens as the motion-picture industry exerts, it is not unnatural—in fact, it is very logical—that subversive and undemocratic forces should attempt to use this medium for un-American purposes." Furthermore, he claimed to already have a list of movies that contained un-American, pro-communist messages. No one had seen the list, and this made Hollywood executives nervous.

The previous May, Thomas and fellow representatives John McDowell and Richard Nixon had been in Los Angeles to interview fourteen witnesses in closed-door hearings. Most of the witnesses were members of the Motion Picture Alliance for the Preservation of American Ideals, which aimed to remove communists from the film industry. It had been formed in 1944 by a conservative group of Hollywood anti-communists and was supported by the movie studios. The organization's members included movie moguls, producers, directors, screenwriters, and

Left: On September 21, 1947, Chairman J. Parnell Thomas released a statement to newspapers that included the names of the people to whom he had sent subpoenas to appear before the House Committee on Un-American Activities. It included both friendly and unfriendly witnesses. The statement was not intended to be an indication of anybody's patriotism, but it was indeed the chairman's first volley against suspected communists in Hollywood.

By Authority of the House of Representatives of the Congress of the United States of America

To ROBERT E. CLARK, United States Marshal

You are hereby commanded to summon LESTER COLE

to be and appear before the UN-AMERICAN ACTIVITIES

Committee of the House of Representatives of the United States, of which the Hon.

J. PARNELL THOMAS of New Jersey is chairman.

in their chamber in the city of Washington, on October 23rd, 1947

, at the hour of 10:30 A.M.

then and there to testify touching matters of inquiry committed to said Committee; and he is not to depart without leave of said Committee.

Herein fail not, and make return of this summons.

Witness my hand and the seal of the House of Representatives of the United States, at the city of Washington, this 18th day of September, 19 47

Chairman.

Attest:

Clerk.

Lester Cole described feeling "fear, chaos, and uncertainty" when he received this summons, signed by J. Parnell Thomas, to appear before the House Committee on Un-American Activities.

Lester Cole's notice that he was to appear before the House Committee on Un-American Activities on October 31, 1947, instead of October 23.

actors, such as Gary Cooper, Clark Gable, Robert Taylor, and Ginger Rogers. Thomas called these witnesses *friendly* because they were "volunteers of information" and their "Americanism . . . [was] . . . not questioned." Surprisingly, Nixon, a fledgling congressman elected in 1946 primarily by falsely connecting his opponent to communist organizations, had little to say to these witnesses. As for Thomas and McDowell, they did not question what motivated them to point their fingers at others in the film community. Among those the friendly witnesses accused of communism were the nineteen men who were holed up in the Shoreham Hotel on the night of October 19. Were the accusations

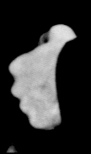

Chairman J. Parnell Thomas (second from left) and members of the House Committee on Un-American Activities. From left, Richard B. Vail, John McDowell, Robert E. Stripling, and Richard M. Nixon. Thomas would eventually be fined and sentenced to prison for congressional payroll fraud.

M.P.A.

THE MOTION PICTURE ALLIANCE

for

THE PRESERVATION OF AMERICAN IDEALS

STATEMENT OF PRINCIPLES

> *"We, even we here, hold the power and bear the responsibility. We shall nobly save, or meanly lose, the last, best hope on earth."* — Abraham Lincoln.

We believe in, and like, the American way of life; the liberty and freedom which generations before us have fought to create and preserve; the freedom to speak, to think, to live, to worship, to work and to govern ourselves, as individuals, as free men; the right to succeed or fail as free men, according to the measure of our ability and our strength.

Believing in these things, we find ourselves in sharp revolt against a rising tide of Communism, Fascism and kindred beliefs, that seek by subversive means to undermine and change this way of life; groups that have forfeited their right to exist in this country of ours, because they seek to achieve their change by means other than the vested procedure of the ballot and to deny the right of the majority opinion of the people to rule.

In our special field of motion pictures, we resent the growing impression that this industry is made up of, and dominated by, Communists, radicals and crack-pots. We believe that we represent the vast majority of the people who serve this great medium of expression. But unfortunately it has been an unorganized majority. This has been almost inevitable. The very love of freedom, of the rights of the individual, make this great majority reluctant to organize. But now we must, or we shall meanly lose "the last, best hope on earth."

As Americans, we have no new plan to offer. We want no new plan, we want only to defend against its enemies that which is our priceless heritage; that freedom which has given man, in this country, the fullest life and the richest expression the world has ever known; that system which, in the present emergency, has fathered an effort that, more than any other single factor, will make possible the winning of this war.

As members of the motion picture industry, we must face and accept an especial responsibility. Motion pictures are inescapably one of the world's greatest forces for influencing public thought and opinion, both at home and abroad. In this fact lies solemn obligation. We refuse to permit the effort of Communist, Fascist, and other totalitarian-minded groups to pervert this powerful medium into an instrument for the dissemination of un-American ideas and beliefs. We pledge ourselves to fight, with every means at our organized command, any effort of any group or individual, to divert the loyalty of the screen from the free America that gave it birth. And to dedicate our own work, in the fullest possible measure, to the presentation of the American scene, its standards and its freedoms, its beliefs and its ideals, as we know them and believe in them.

The Motion Picture Alliance for the Preservation of American Ideals believed in many of the same things that more progressive groups embraced, but its members had a different perspective. They didn't think that communists or fascists had the freedom to exist in the United States.

28

of the friendly witnesses based on a legitimate concern for the political well-being of the U.S.? Were they payback for an old slight? Might they have been the result of professional jealousy or, perhaps, an effort to bust up the workers' unions? Their claims were not challenged by Thomas, McDowell, or Nixon, but instead accepted as fact.

Now that the hearings were in progress, Thomas asserted, "There is no question that there are Communists in Hollywood." Before he could instruct the first witness to be called, though, Robert W. Kenny rose to speak: "Mr. Chairman, I am attorney for the 19 subpenaed witnesses, as is Mr. Bartley Crum. You recall that we submitted a telegram yesterday on a motion to quash [withdraw the subpoenas]." Kenny hoped to argue that the purpose of the committee—to inquire into people's personal political beliefs and associations—was unconstitutional. Thomas told the former attorney general of the state of California that he would have his chance to present his argument when the witnesses were called to testify.

Bartley C. Crum then spoke up: "May we ask if we have a right to cross-examine?"

"You may not ask one more thing at this time," Thomas said. He quickly told Robert E. Stripling, the permanent secretary and chief investigator of the committee, to swear in the first witness.

During that week, witnesses friendly to the committee were allowed to accuse those whom they suspected were communists without offering any real evidence supporting the charge. Their accusations were based on suspicions, rumors, or gut feelings rather than actual facts. They also named films they believed were communist propaganda. Sometimes their impressions were based on details such as a wealthy individual or banker being

29

portrayed in a film as corrupt, or even on a snippet of dialogue. Lela Rogers, the mother of actress Ginger Rogers, reported that *None but the Lonely Heart* was communistic because a character said, "You are not going to get me to work here and squeeze pennies out of little people poorer than I am." Crum and the other attorneys believed that cross-examination was essential to defending their clients. They also believed that the hearings were, in everything but name, an American trial complete with accusers and a judge—Thomas, the committee, and public opinion. What the hearings lacked, however, was any requirement to follow the rules that governed all U.S. courts of law.

* * *

It was a week before the attorneys for the nineteen were able to raise their concerns before the committee again. On Monday, October 27, screenwriter John Howard Lawson was called as the first unfriendly witness. The "unfriendly" label had been pinned on the nineteen men by the *Hollywood Reporter*, an entertainment publication, because they had vowed not to cooperate with the committee. These witnesses viewed the committee's questions as unconstitutional, a violation of their First Amendment rights. Their attorneys based this argument on the Supreme Court decision in *Kilbourn v. Thompson*, which ruled that "Congress may conduct investigations only for the purpose of gathering information relevant to contemplated future legislation" and may not investigate "the private affairs of individuals."

Before Lawson could take the witness stand, Kenny rose to address Thomas: "Mr. Chairman, if you will recall, at the outset of this hearing Mr. Crum and I made a motion to quash the subpenas addressed to Mr. Lawson and some 18 other witnesses whom we represent. You indicated at that time that this would be the appropriate occasion at which to present our arguments for the quashing of the subpenas, on the ground that this committee is illegal and unconstitutional."

Thomas suspended the hearing to consider Kenny's argument, but Crum interrupted: "Mr. Chairman, may I ask that you consider our motion to cross-examine—" Chairman Thomas cut him off, instructing the committee to leave the room.

When the HUAC returned less than twenty minutes later, Thomas gaveled the hearing to order. "Mr. Kenny," he began, "this is the unanimous decision of this [committee]. . . . No committee of Congress has the right to establish it [*sic*] own legality or constitutionality." The committee wasn't about to put itself out of business, especially not in front of the newsreel cameras and reporters. Stripling was ordered once more to call Lawson to testify.

For the second time that morning, Crum requested that the attorneys for the nineteen be allowed to cross-examine the witnesses from the previous week's testimony. Thomas pounded his gavel to silence Crum and said, "The request is denied."

Lawson, after being sworn in, asked if he could read his prepared statement. The week before, friendly witnesses had been allowed to read lengthy statements, often without interruption— unless the committee wanted to clarify points it wished to stress in front of the whirring cameras and furiously scribbling reporters. According to Gordon Kahn, "A copy [of Lawson's statement] was handed up to Thomas, who no more than glanced at it than he thrust it away from him, aghast. The other members of the committee looked just as horrified."

"I don't care to read any more of the statement," Thomas said. "The statement will not be read. I read the first line."

Lawson protested, saying, "You refuse to allow me to make a statement on my rights as an American citizen."

"I refuse you to make the statement," the chairman argued, "because of the first sentence in your statement."

What was it that so irritated Thomas to the point of shouting? Lawson's statement questioned the constitutionality and legality of the HUAC itself: "For a week, this Committee has conducted an illegal and indecent trial of American citizens, whom the Committee has selected to be publicly pilloried and smeared." Apparently, Thomas had one rule for friendly witnesses and another for those who questioned the committee's authority or cast it in an unfavorable light.

Stripling continued with the routine questions asked of every witness—name, date and place of birth, occupation, and whether he was at the hearings in response to a subpoena. Then he changed course, asking Lawson, "Are you a member of the Screen Writers Guild?"

Throughout the first week of the hearings, witness after witness had cast the Screen Writers Guild as a hotbed of communism. Jack Warner, vice president in charge of production at Warner Bros., was the first to point his finger at writers, saying that those with un-American leanings existed "mostly in the writing division." But there was more to the story. The Screen Writers Guild was the writers' recognized union, and it had negotiated favorable contracts with studio bosses for its members. It was pushing for writers to keep more control over their work. Conservative studio heads considered its demands too extreme. They had retaliated with a rival union, Screen Playwrights, Inc., which, not surprisingly, demanded less and was more to the moguls' liking. Although they finally agreed in 1938 to recognize the Screen

Writers Guild as the only union authorized to negotiate for writers, the studio executives wanted to be rid of it. Smearing it as a communist-controlled guild, or union, in 1947 was one way to diminish its influence and bring about its end.

Lawson's response to Stripling's question started a verbal exchange, with each man interrupting the other.

The screenwriter began, "The raising of any question here in regard to membership, political beliefs, or affiliation—"

"Mr. Chairman—" Stripling interrupted.

"Is absolutely beyond the powers of this committee."

"Mr. Chairman—"

"But—"

When Thomas's gavel hammered out his disapproval, Lawson finally answered, "It is a matter of public record that I am a member of the Screen Writers Guild."

In fact, Lawson had been a founding member of the guild and its first president. His comment was met with a burst of applause from the spectators in the Caucus Room. In fact, most of the nineteen witnesses were screenwriters and members of the guild. The outburst annoyed the chairman, and he scolded the audience.

Lawson, still bristling from not being able to read his statement, threw down the gauntlet: "I am not on trial here, Mr. Chairman. This committee is on trial here before the American people. Let us get that straight."

Thomas, if annoyed before, was downright hostile now. He threatened to remove Lawson from the stand and to cite him for contempt of Congress, a charge that could carry a fine and up to one year in prison.

"I am glad you have made it perfectly clear that you are going to threaten and intimidate the witnesses, Mr. Chairman," Lawson said. At that, Thomas's angry gavel strikes ricocheted throughout the chamber.

Lawson relented, answering several of the investigator's questions, but only because this information—such as whether he was a member of the Screen Writers Guild or if he had written this or that movie—was already in the public record. Finally, Stripling got to the question he'd been leading up to from the beginning of his interrogation, the heart of the hearings. "Mr. Lawson," he asked, "are you now, or have you ever been a member of the Communist Party of the United States?"

J. Parnell Thomas (left), chairman of the House Committee on Un-American Activities, shakes hands with Jack Warner, vice president in charge of production at Warner Bros. Warner was a friendly witness.

John Howard Lawson leans in to the microphone to lash out at Chairman J. Parnell Thomas about Americanism, the First Amendment, and the Constitution of the United States before he is told to leave the witness chair.

THE GOVERNMENT INVESTIGATES ITS OWN CITIZENS

The 1947 hearings held by the Committee on Un-American Activities (also called the Thomas Committee, for its chairman, J. Parnell Thomas) were not the first. The government had looked into the political leanings of private citizens and organizations many times before. Following the Russian Revolution of 1917, which had resulted in the overthrow of Czar Nicholas II and the assassination of the royal family in 1918, a communist scare swept the United States as Congress and American industrialists worried that workers might rise up to unionize and revolt against their employers, as they had done in Russia.

American laborers were generally poorly paid, yet they were creating wealth for their bosses and business investors. They often worked in unsafe conditions and had no protections if they became injured. As in Russia before the revolution, a chasm existed between the haves and the have-nots. A special Senate committee—dubbed the Overman Committee after its chairman, Democratic senator Lee Overman of North Carolina—was set up in 1919. The committee investigated the threat posed to American labor by Russian, or communist, propaganda. Its main success

The Communist Party USA was popular during the 1930s and 1940s largely because of its emphasis on workers and racial and social equality during a time when the U.S. economy was shaky and prejudice was common. Many thought that an American version of the communist revolution in Russia would make things better in the United States.

was in painting communism and communists as barbaric because of the violence that had occurred during the Russian Revolution.

Despite American workers' dissatisfaction with their working conditions, union membership in the U.S. actually declined in the 1920s. One reason for this was a series of raids, conducted by the U.S. Department of Justice in 1919 and 1920, that cracked down on the labor movement with searches, arrests, deportations, and other civil rights violations. Newspapers also often portrayed unions as a threat to the country's social stability. Membership carried with it a risk that some workers weren't willing to take.

In 1929, the stock market crashed, throwing the economy of the United States and much of the world into the Great Depression. Massive unemployment, homelessness, and hunger resulted. Some worried that the free enterprise system and American democracy were on the verge of collapse and that an alternative political system—communism—might offer hope to the millions of desperate people.

The following year, Representative Hamilton Fish III, a Republican from New York, proposed a special committee to investigate communist activities in America—especially their influence on the timber industry. He believed that Russian imports of lumber were hurting American business interests. Traveling across the country and holding hearings in major cities, the Fish Committee learned that communism posed a triple threat to the country: (1) political, as it advocated the overthrow of the government; (2) moral, since communism was atheistic and didn't recognize any god or religion; and (3) economic, because it embraced the idea of government-owned industry over private enterprise. Although Fish was wrong about Russian imports threatening the timber trade, his rhetoric "inspired

fear and paranoia." Moreover, the representative recommended strengthening immigration and deportation laws as a means to rid the country of the communist threat.

The House of Representatives established another special committee to investigate subversive activities in 1934. The McCormack-Dickstein Committee—named after its chairman, John W. McCormack, a Democrat from Massachusetts, and its vice chairman, Samuel Dickstein, a Democrat from New York— was a reaction to the overthrow of several foreign governments in favor of fascism or communism. (Fascism is an authoritarian

The McCormack-Dickstein Committee at a hearing in Washington, DC. They are, from left to right, Samuel Dickstein (New York), Ulysses S. Guyer (Kansas), Chairman John McCormack (Massachusetts), and Charles Kramer (California). Soviet records uncovered in 1999 indicated that Dickstein was a mole, or secret agent, of the Russian government while serving in Congress.

political regime, sometimes racist in its views, that is headed by a dictator who believes his or her country is better than any other nation.) In public and closed-door hearings, the committee collected more than four thousand pages of documentation on individuals and organizations that allegedly "worked to establish in the United States policies followed by the Nazis in Germany, the Fascists in Italy, and the Communists in Russia." The committee soon fell out of favor in Congress, however, because of Dickstein's imposing personality.

Although the McCormack-Dickstein Committee had lost its influence, Congress continued to worry about how world affairs might play out in the United States. As Adolf Hitler exerted his power over Germany in the 1930s and threatened its neighbors, and as communism took hold in countries outside of Russia, members of the House of Representatives grew even more concerned that German and Russian undercover agents might have infiltrated the U.S. for the purpose of strengthening pro-Nazi and pro-communist groups here. On May 26, 1938, the House authorized a new, seven-member committee to explore anti-American propaganda in the U.S.—the Special Committee on Un-American Activities, also called the Dies Committee, for its chairman, Representative Martin Dies Jr., a Democrat from Texas. Its job was to look into subversive teachings and messages, determine how they were dispersed to the public, and learn whether they were the work of foreign agents or U.S. citizens. The committee's main purpose was to collect information that would help Congress craft laws to protect the U.S. government and the people it served from these threats.

Though a Democrat like President Franklin Delano Roosevelt, the conservative Dies was a longtime foe of the president's

Representative Martin Dies Jr. of Texas turned to radio to inspire the nation to attack communists, President Franklin D. Roosevelt, and others he felt were attempting to discredit his committee.

progressive, forward-thinking policies. Roosevelt, elected in 1932 during the Great Depression, when at least one-quarter of America's labor force was unemployed, initiated several plans aimed at stabilizing the economy and putting people back to work. These programs were known as the New Deal. They included the Civilian Conservation Corps, which put people to work building structures and trails in the country's parks; the Public Works Administration, which funded the construction of airports, electricity-generating dams, schools, and hospitals; and the Works Progress Administration, or WPA (renamed the Work Projects Administration in 1939), which employed mostly unskilled workers, as well as unemployed actors, writers, and musicians.

It was the WPA's Federal Theatre Project (FTP) and Federal Writers' Project that came under the scrutiny of the Dies Committee, especially committee member J. Parnell Thomas. Thomas called the FTP "a branch of the communistic organization . . . [and] one more link in the vast and unparalleled New Deal propaganda machine," and he claimed it was "infested with radicals from top to bottom." According to Thomas, "Practically every play presented under the auspices of the project either centered on a plot sympathetic to the cause of communism or serves as a vehicle for the propagation of New Deal theories." One WPA official accused the Dies Committee of ignoring the "American tradition of fair play and unbiased investigation."

Not satisfied investigating New Deal programs and accusing Roosevelt of being soft on communism, the committee set its sights further afield—to Hollywood's moviemaking business. The world was in chaos in the 1930s, with a global economic depression brought on by the 1929 stock market crash, the rise of Hitler's Nazi Party in Germany, Europe on the brink of war,

Representative Martin Dies Jr. (right) interviews actor Humphrey Bogart (left) as a special House Committee on Un-American Activities looked into communist propaganda in America. Sitting next to Dies is the committee's chief investigator Robert E. Stripling. Also pictured is committee investigator James Steedman.

and a civil war in Spain. Many in the movie industry lent their celebrity and financial support to causes such as the Hollywood Anti-Nazi League. Some had abandoned careers to join the Abraham Lincoln Brigade, which fought for a democratic Spain in that country's civil war. The Dies Committee assigned investigators to look into these organizations and their members. It wasn't long before the committee accused them of being communist fronts—groups that claimed to support one cause while actually raising money for another, such as the Communist Party.

Hollywood fought back. Author and screenwriter Donald Ogden Stewart said it was unfortunate that the Dies Committee had "adopted the practice of making accusations without possessing the facts to substantiate them" and called the investigation "a threat to democracy." Author, screenwriter, and humorist Dorothy Parker turned serious to say, "It is an ominous sign that the Dies investigating committee has adopted the practice of making accusations without possessing the facts to substantiate them. When Hitler is mobilizing a million men on the Czechoslovakia border [now two countries, Slovakia and the Czech Republic] . . . these charges leveled at an organization devoted to the task of combating Nazism are in themselves a threat to democracy." The organization's members accused the investigators of being un-American, while producer John W. Considine Jr. claimed, "We are busy making motion pictures here—we haven't time to act any 'ism,' Nazi, Fascist or Red." Even President Roosevelt eventually observed that the Dies Committee's actions "may defeat the ends of justice." Nonetheless, Dies and his committee continued to find subversive elements everywhere. After Japan bombed Pearl Harbor on

Above: Screenwriter Donald Ogden Stewart claimed the Dies Committee was accusing individuals and organizations of communism without any evidence, especially the Hollywood Anti-Nazi League. He is best remembered for co-writing the screenplay for *The Philadelphia Story* (1940).

Below: Writer Dorothy Parker left humor behind when she accused the Dies Committee of being a threat to democracy.

December 7, 1941, Dies called for all people of Japanese ancestry to be moved inland five hundred miles from the west coast and held in concentration camps, while J. Parnell Thomas claimed, without evidence, that Japanese Americans were a dangerous division of the Japanese army.

In January 1945, the Dies Committee was changed to a standing committee of the House of Representatives now called the House Committee on Un-American Activities. Dies had not run for reelection in 1944 and was replaced as chairman by Edward Hart, a Democrat from New Jersey.

The investigations into the New Deal programs and the Hollywood movie business continued under President Harry S. Truman following Roosevelt's death in April 1945, but mostly they were given a rest until after World War II ended later that year.

3

TAKING THE STAND; TAKING A STAND

On the morning of October 27, 1947, John Howard Lawson was scheduled to be the third witness, but was caught off guard when he was called first.

Robert E. Stripling fired off the question that lay at the heart of the hearings: "Mr. Lawson, are you now, or have you ever been a member of the Communist Party of the United States?" The question was asked in this way because "in the early days of the Martin Dies Committee . . . the question had simply been, Are you a member of the Communist Party of the United States? As a countermeasure, the Party adopted a rule that automatically cancelled a Communist's membership the moment the question was asked. He could then answer 'No' without perjuring himself." If Stripling expected a simple yes or no response from Lawson, he was in for an awakening.

Lawson, like most of the eighteen other unfriendly witnesses, was indeed a communist, and the committee was well aware of it. Although a gifted writer and one who was born into money, he wasn't well liked in the film capital. "His personality . . . often jangled nerves in a Hollywood otherwise known for insecurity." Some considered him to be a traitor to his class. "In a nation

Ten of the Hollywood nineteen and their attorneys. Front row, from left: Herbert Biberman, Martin Popper (attorney), Robert W. Kenny (attorney), Albert Maltz, and Lester Cole. Second row, from left: Dalton Trumbo, John Howard Lawson, Alvah Bessie, and Samuel Ornitz. Back row, from left: Ring Lardner Jr., Edward Dmytryk, and Adrian Scott.

not adverse [*sic*] to anti-Semitism," or prejudice against Jews, Lawson was Jewish, and this contributed to people's dislike of him. His son Jeffrey described him an aloof, angry "man who seldom spoke to me, who was not affectionate." Perhaps Lawson's aloofness and anger stemmed from having grown up with an absent father himself.

Lawson was head of the Communist Party in the Hollywood area. To trap him in a lie at the outset of interrogating the nineteen may have been the reason Thomas changed the order of the witnesses. At the direction of the committee, a team of investigators, mostly former agents of the Federal Bureau of Investigation (FBI), had compiled files on all of the witnesses. They were followed wherever they went, and they suspected that their phones were bugged, or monitored by listening devices. Lawson had to be careful with his answer. If he said no, the committee would most certainly charge him with perjury, based on evidence contained in the files, and a prison sentence would likely follow. If he answered yes, the committee would demand that he name others who also were communists.

Lawson ultimately responded, "In framing my answer to that question I must emphasize the points that I have raised before." He then went on the attack, accusing the HUAC of attempting, through its questions, to gain control over the motion picture business and to invade the basic rights of American citizens. Both Representative John McDowell and Stripling objected. Chairman Thomas loudly banged his gavel, which he continued to do throughout Lawson's remarks. As Lester Cole later observed, "It soon became a shouting match."

"The question here relates not only to the question of my membership in any political organization," Lawson continued,

50

"but this committee is attempting to establish the right . . . which has been historically denied to any committee of this sort, to invade the rights and privileges and immunity of American citizens, whether they be Protestant, Methodist, Jewish, or Catholic, whether they be Republicans or Democrats or anything else." Despite the hammering gavel and Thomas's protests, Lawson continued to lob accusations at the chairman, accusing him of using the same techniques that Hitler had used in Germany "in order to create a scare here . . . in order to create an entirely false atmosphere in which this hearing is conducted . . . in order that you can then smear the motion-picture industry, and you can proceed to the press, to any form of communication in this country. The Bill of Rights was established precisely to prevent the operation of any committee which could invade the basic rights of Americans."

Stripling continued repeating that Lawson wasn't answering the question put to him, even as Thomas exercised his gavel. But Lawson was far from through. He wasn't finished teaching his American government lesson to the legislators on the stage. "If you want to know . . . about the perjury that has been committed here and the perjury that is planned . . . you [will] permit me and my attorneys to bring in here the witnesses that testified last week and you [will] permit us to cross-examine these witnesses."

Thomas finally ran out of patience. "We are going to get the answer to that question," he threatened, "if we have to stay here for a week. Are you a member . . . of the Communist Party?"

Lawson remained firm in his belief that he was under no obligation to answer the chairman's question in any way but his own. "It is unfortunate and tragic," he shouted, "that I have to teach this committee the basic principles of American—"

"[Lawson] was choked off at the last syllable by the gavel and Thomas' repetition of the $64 question," Gordon Kahn later wrote. (Kahn called it the $64 question after a popular radio game show that awarded winners $64 as the top prize. The phrase was commonly used to mean any question of great importance, and this question lay at the heart of the HUAC hearings. Asking about the Screen Writers Guild, which Stripling had done earlier, was secondary and thus called the $32 question.)

With his face flushed red, Thomas, hammering his gavel, bellowed, "That is not the question. That is not the question. The question is: Have you ever been a member of the Communist Party?"

Lawson continued to attempt to answer the question in his own way, which did not include the simple yes or no that Thomas was demanding. The chairman wanted either a confirmation of what its file on Lawson suggested—and, as a result, the names of other communists in Hollywood—or a denial. A denial, of course, would lead to the charge of perjury. Either one would be an admission by Lawson that the committee had a right to ask about the private thoughts and associations of American citizens.

Thomas again took to exercising his gavel. "Excuse the witness—" he demanded. When Lawson attempted to object, Thomas cut him off, saying, "Stand away from the stand—"

Lawson wasn't finished lecturing the chairman. Defiant, he shouted, "I have written Americanism for many years, and I shall continue to fight for the Bill of Rights, which you are trying to destroy."

Thomas, now enraged, ordered officers to "take this man away from the stand." The audience both applauded and booed. After scolding them, the chairman told Stripling to proceed.

Actor Larry Parks (left) and producer Adrian Scott listen to testimony at the opening session of the House Committee on Un-American Activities on October 20, 1947.

The next person to take the stand turned out to be an investigator for the committee, Louis J. Russell. Before the newsreel cameras, the newspaper reporters, and the spectators in the Caucus Room, Stripling read from Russell's file on Lawson. It showed the connections Lawson had to the Communist Party. He had written several articles for the *Daily Worker*, which Stripling identified as the party's "official organ."

Stripling then turned to Russell and asked, "What did your investigation disclose?"

Russell replied, "During the course of my investigation . . . we were furnished—or I was—with copies of Communist Party registration cards. . . . One of those cards bears the number '47275' and is made out in the name of John Howard Lawson."

After this revelation, Stripling took over, reading from a nine-page, single-spaced file containing evidence condemning Lawson as a communist. It included the statement of a witness, a former communist, who had seen Lawson at a Communist Party meeting. Other evidence of his affiliation was that he had defended the party in a public speech, donated to the party or to organizations thought to be fronts for it, and shown an interest in the USSR. Finally, an article in the *Hollywood Citizen-News* said that Lawson had proposed a plan to examine the backgrounds of HUAC members and investigators. This last bit of information was important. Attacking the accusers was an alleged tactic of communists. McDowell interrupted to ask that it be read again, just in case the newsreel cameras and reporters had failed to grasp the significance of it. Although the screenwriter's prepared statement hadn't been placed into the public record of the hearings, Russell's file on Lawson was.

About belonging to the Communist Party, one of the nineteen unfriendly witnesses, Ring Lardner Jr., later offered some insight. "Neither I nor any of my friends in the party wanted the U.S. remodeled along Soviet lines," he wrote. "We deplored the absence of free elections [in Russia], the cult of personality that surrounded Stalin [the Soviet leader], and the general atmosphere of regimentation. . . . In America, we believed, the conversion to a rational economic system would be accomplished peacefully at the polls. We also expected that . . . Russia would become more, rather than less, democratic, and the failure of that to happen

"Thomas Committee Members Beating and chaining a man labeled 'Movies'"—Studio executives were afraid that the House Committee on Un-American Activities wanted to put a straitjacket on Hollywood and censor its films. Equally worried were artists of all stripes, members of the press, and writers for radio. In the beginning, however, many stood by silently until they, too, were swept up by the committee's investigations.

was beginning to stir doubts among some of us even as we faced the committee." Like Lawson, Lardner was a screenwriter and belonged to the Screen Writers Guild.

Indeed, doubt was beginning to infect many of the witnesses. Movie director Edward Dmytryk wrote in his memoir, "It was unnecessary for Lawson to identify himself as a communist." His attack proved that he was. Following Lawson's performance,

Dmytryk felt a sinking feeling that the hearings would not go well for any of them.

Eric Johnston, president of the Motion Picture Association of America (MPAA), was next on the stand. The MPAA had been formed in 1922 by the major studios to promote and defend the industry. Its primary purpose was to ensure that offensive materials didn't make it into films and to fight government interference in filmmaking. Johnston had assured Robert W. Kenny, attorney for the nineteen, that he and the MPAA would "never be a party to anything as un-American as a blacklist." A blacklist in this case would be a list of people the motion picture moguls considered unemployable because they might trigger a backlash from the movie-going public that would cut into the studios' profits. But a blacklist would not only affect individuals' ability to get a job; it would also make anyone whose name appeared on it a pariah, an outcast in society.

Johnston's job was to defend the studios. He began by saying, "A damaging impression of Hollywood has spread all over the country as a result of last week's hearings. . . . From some of it [the friendly testimony] the public will get the idea that Hollywood is running over with Communists and communism." His comment made the committee members sit up, and it immediately put them on the defensive, but they let him continue. As he did, he complained that Chairman Thomas had condemned the entire industry by failing to make public a list of movies the committee claimed contained communist propaganda. It was impossible for the film industry to defend itself against a generalization. Then, almost as an afterthought, he touched on the idea of a blacklist. Johnston obviously was less concerned about the fate of the nineteen witnesses than he was about the people paying his salary. "Our freedoms," he offered, "would become empty and meaningless without the keystone of our freedom arch— freedom of speech—freedom to speak, to hear, and to see." Before Johnston stepped away from the witness stand, he offered the committee some cautionary advice: "It . . . is getting dangerously easy to call a man a Communist without proof or even reasonable suspicion. . . . We are not willing to give up our freedoms to save our freedoms."

Indeed, from its earliest beginnings in the 1930s, the Committee on Un-American Activities had been unpopular and the target of criticism for its invasion into the privacy of American citizens and its unfair, authoritarian hearing procedures. Now, in 1947, opposition to the committee had only grown. Senator Claude Pepper, a Democrat from Florida, referred to the Thomas committee as a group of "crypto-fascists." The conference of eight hundred people where Pepper was speaking unanimously called to eliminate the HUAC.

Pepper's criticism was joined over the weekend by a group of Hollywood film stars—"twenty-five prominent movie personages" and friends of the nineteen—who had flown to Washington to oppose "the inquiry of the Committee on Un-American Activities." These members of the Committee for the First Amendment (CFA), a progressive group in opposition to the HUAC and its tactics, bought time on the American Broadcasting Company's radio network to air a nationwide program "denouncing the inquiry as an abridgement of free expression." The CFA's production included Hollywood celebrities as well as "four democratic senators, Elbert D. Thomas of Utah, Harley M. Kilgore of West Virginia, Claude Pepper of Florida and Glen H. Taylor of Idaho." During the program, actress Myrna Loy stressed

Lauren Bacall and Humphrey Bogart lead a delegation of Hollywood film stars into the U.S. Capitol on October 27, 1947, as the second week of testimony before the House Committee on Un-American Activities gets under way. Behind Bacall and Bogart are June Havoc and Danny Kaye. Paul Henreid is walking behind Havoc. The other people are unidentified.

the group's main theme: "We question the right of Congress to ask any man what he thinks on political issues." Film producer and director John Huston scolded the HUAC for producing only one piece of legislation in all its years of existence that addressed subversive activity—"and that was rejected as unconstitutional." And actress and singer Judy Garland urged listeners to write to their congressional representatives to protest the inquiry.

Additionally, a *New York Times* article written by Arthur Krock condemned the Thomas Committee and the committees that had come before it as "abusing witnesses, flagrantly disregarding private rights and tearing up the Constitution." In California, "a group of . . . scientists" called for Congress to "legislate the Un-American Activities Committee out of existence." Among those condemning the committee was the Nobel Prize–winning chemist Linus Pauling. In a signed statement, the scientists said that the committee's methods would "intimidate and stifle all cultural and social thought except that approved by the committee itself." Even communist Ukraine got in on the act, calling the inquiry a "persecution of those who 'dare to say one friendly word about the Soviet Union.'"

If the HUAC had thought Lawson was a difficult witness, they didn't know what lay in store for them from Dalton Trumbo, "a veritable ring-tailed tiger" and the next unfriendly witness. Trumbo later wrote that he became a communist not so much for the party line, but because he wanted to be with his friends, to be surrounded by stimulating conversation. Married and the father of three, he was an isolationist who had opposed the United States' entry into WWII. Lardner once described him as "a determined indoorsman" who "liked to write in the bathtub,

Committee for the First Amendment

ARTICLE I.

Congress shall make no law respecting an establishment of religion, or prohibiting the free exercise thereof; or abridging the freedom of speech or of the press; or the right of the people peaceably to assemble and to petition the Government for a redress of grievances.

—The Constitution of the United States.

Larry Adler
Stephen Morehouse Avery

Geraldine Brooks
Roma Burton
Lauren Bacall
Barbara Bentley
Leonardo Bercovici
Leonard Bernstein
DeWitt Bodeen
Humphrey Bogart
Ann and Mort Braus
Richard Brooks

Jerome Chodorov
Cheryl Crawford
Louis Calhern
Frank Callender
Eddie Cantor
McClure Capps
Warren Cowan
Richard Conte
Norman Corwin
Tom Carlyle

Agnes DeMille
Delmer Daves
Donald Davies
Spencer Davies
Donald Davis
Armand Deutsch
Walter Doniger
I. A. L. Diamond
Muni Diamond
Kirk Douglas
Jay Dratler
Philip Dunne
Howard Duff

Paul Draper

Phoebe and Henry Ephron
Julius Epstein
Philip Epstein
Charles Einfeld

Sylvia Fine
Henry Fonda
Melvin Frank

Irwin Gelsey
Benny Goodman
Ava Gardner
Sheridan Gibney
Paulette Goddard
Michael Gordon
Jay Goldberg
Jesse J. Goldburg

Moss Hart
Rita Hayworth
David Hopkins
Katharine Hepburn
Paul Henreid
Van Heflin
John Huston
Walter Huston
John Houseman
Marsha Hunt
Joseph Hoffman
Uta Hagen

Robert L. Joseph

George Kaufman
Norman Krasna
Herbert Kline

Michel Kraike
Isobel Katleman
Arthur Kober
Evelyn Keyes
Gene Kelly
Danny Kaye
J. Richard Kennedy
Harry Kurnitz
Fred Kohlmar

Canada Lee
Anatole Litvak
Burt Lancaster
Herbert Clyde Lewis
Arthur Lubin
Mary Loos
Myrna Loy

Burgess Meredith
Richard Maibaum
David Miller
Frank L. Moss
Margo
Dorothy McGuire
Ivan Moffatt
Josef Mischel
Dorothy Matthews

Lorie Niblo
N. Richard Nash
Doris Nolan

George Oppenheimer

Ernest Pascal
Vincent Price
Norman Panama
Marion Parsonnet

Frank Partos
Jean Porter
John Paxton
Bob Presnell, Jr.
Gregory Peck

Harold Rome
Gladys Robinson
Francis Rosenwald
Irving Rubine
Irving Reis
Stanley Rubin
Sylvia Richards
Henry C. Rogers
Lyle Rooks
Norman and Betsy Rose
Robert Ryan

Irwin Shaw
Richard Sale
George Seaton
John Stone
Allan Scott
Barry Sullivan
Shepperd Strudwick
Mrs. Leo Spitz
Theodore Strauss
John and Marti Shelton
Robert Shapiro

Joseph Than
Leo Townsend

Don Victor
Bernard Vorhaus

Billy Wilder
Bill Watters
Jerry Wald
Cornel Wilde

We are arranging for radio broadcasts and other steps to protest the conduct of the Washington hearings. If you wish to volunteer to help us or to contribute money, please wire:

"BILL OF RIGHTS"

CARE OF WESTERN UNION
BEVERLY HILLS, CALIF.

The Committee for the First Amendment—friends and supporters of the nineteen unfriendly witnesses—was made up of Hollywood celebrities. Some would face blacklisting themselves for standing up to J. Parnell Thomas and the House Committee on Un-American Activities, while others eventually would withdraw their support of the witnesses.

pen in one hand, cigarette in the other. His major leisure activity was argument."

Several witnesses during the first week of the hearings had cast a shadow over Trumbo's loyalty to the United States, so he approached the witness stand with a box containing his movie scripts. A number of round canisters holding films he had written were stacked under the witness chair. Like Lawson's before him, Trumbo's statement was passed up to the committee and promptly rejected as "not pertinent to the inquiry." The first few lines of his statement offended Thomas and the other committee members: "As indicated by news dispatches from foreign countries during the past week, the eyes of the world are focused to-day upon the House Committee on Un-American Activities. . . . From what happens during the proceedings, the peoples of the earth will learn by precept and example precisely what America means when her strong voice calls out to the community of nations for freedom of the press, freedom of expression, freedom of conscience, the civil rights of men standing accused before government agencies, the vitality and strength of private enterprise, the inviolable right of every American to think as he wishes, to organize and assemble as he pleases, to vote in secret as he chooses."

Trumbo objected to Thomas's ruling, but the chairman threatened, "If you conduct yourself like the first witness yesterday [Lawson], you won't be given the privilege of being a witness . . . before this committee of Congress." Trumbo didn't consider it a privilege to testify before the HUAC. Like the other witnesses, he had been forced to appear by a subpoena and had to pay his own way to Washington. If he'd ignored the order, Thomas would have charged him with contempt of Congress. Appearing on the witness stand was anything but a privilege.

Thomas ordered Stripling to ask the first question. When Stripling inquired whether Trumbo was a member of the Screen Writers Guild, Trumbo asked if he could submit as evidence into the hearing record two statements, one by a general in the U.S. Army Air Forces and the other by a municipal court judge. These statements addressed the content of Trumbo's work, as well as his character as an American. "I shall ask various questions," Stripling said, directing his remarks to Trumbo, "all of which can be answered 'Yes' or 'No.' If you want to give an explanation after you have made that answer, I feel sure that the committee will agree to that."

Trumbo responded, "Very many questions can be answered 'Yes' or 'No' only by a moron or a slave."

Surprisingly, Thomas agreed with Trumbo, but stipulated that he "should answer the questions."

Having gotten that much out of Thomas, Trumbo promised not to make a speech, but asked if he might introduce into the record "20 scripts . . . so that it may be known what my work is, and what this committee may seek to prevent the American people from seeing in the future."

Stripling didn't like what he was suggesting and objected. The chairman, however, asked how long the scripts were. When Trumbo told him that each was 115 to 170 pages in length, Thomas reached his decision quickly: "Too many pages." This dashed any hope Trumbo may have had about having his scripts, produced films, or character statements placed into the record.

Stripling made another attempt to ask if Trumbo was a member of the Screen Writers Guild.

"Mr. Stripling," Trumbo began, "the rights of American labor to inviolably secret membership lists have been won in this country."

Thomas accused Trumbo of speechmaking, and it fell to him to try a third, fourth, and fifth time to get a yes or no answer out of the screenwriter: "Can't you answer: Are you a member of the Screen Writers Guild, by saying 'Yes' or 'No,' or I think so, or maybe, or something like that?"

"Mr. Chairman," Trumbo replied, "I would not consider it a disgrace to be a member of a labor union. . . . But labor unions have the right to secrecy of their membership lists. . . . This question is designed to a specific purpose. First, to identify me with the Screen Writers Guild; secondly, to seek to identify me with the Communist Party and thereby destroy that guild—"

Thomas interrupted, pounding his gavel. According to Gordon Kahn, "Somebody in the audience said, in a loud whisper, 'He's got something!'" At that, Thomas became enraged. Continuing to pound his gavel, he shouted, "Excuse the witness—"

But the chief investigator hadn't asked Trumbo "the $64 question." After a moment's confusion over whether Trumbo was or was not dismissed, Stripling asked: "Are you now, or have you ever been a member of the Communist Party?"

Trumbo replied, "You must have some reason for asking this question—"

"Yes, we do." It was McDowell, speaking for the committee.

"I believe I have the right to be confronted with any evidence which supports this question. I should like to see what you have," Trumbo said.

The chairman, who had rarely smiled over the course of the

week's hearings, grinned like the Cheshire cat and said, "Well, you will, pretty soon."

This comment was met with laughter and applause.

Banging his gavel again, the chairman said, "The witness is excused."

Trumbo wasn't about to be dismissed without getting in another word. Over the sound of Thomas's gavel, he said, "This is the beginning—"

"Just a minute—" Thomas interrupted.

"Of an American concentration camp."

But it was Thomas, not Trumbo, who had the last word. "This is typical Communist tactics," he shouted. "This is typical Communist tactics."

Stripling then pulled out a sheaf of papers containing "nine pages," including an article from the *Hollywood Reporter*, in which Trumbo was asked if he was a communist. "Mr. Trumbo has never answered that challenge," Stripling said. He continued to read thirty-nine points, all of them signaling that Trumbo had connections to the Communist Party.

In case there was still any doubt about Trumbo's political associations, Thomas summarized them for the newsreel cameras and reporters: "The evidence presented before this committee concerning Dalton Trumbo clearly indicates that he is an active Communist Party member."

Screenwriter Albert Maltz followed Trumbo on the witness stand. Almost immediately, he asked to read a statement. Thomas surprised everyone by allowing it into the record without even looking at it. After thanking the chairman, Maltz read: "I am an American and I believe there is no more proud word in the

vocabulary of man. . . . Whatever I am, America has made me. And I, in turn, possess no loyalty as great as the one I have to this land, to the economic and social welfare of its people, to the perpetuation and development of its democractic [sic] way of life.

"Now at the age of 39, I am commanded to appear before the House Committee on Un-American Activities. For a full week this committee has encouraged an assortment of well-rehearsed witnesses to testify that I and others are subversive and un-American. It has refused us the opportunity that any pickpocket receives in a magistrate's court—the right to cross-examine these witnesses, to refute their testimony, to reveal their motives, their history, and who, exactly, they are. Furthermore it grants these witnesses congressional immunity so that we may not sue them for libel for their slanders."

As he continued to read, it became clear that Maltz was accusing the committee, as had Lawson and Trumbo in their unread statements, of trying to silence opinion. Yet Maltz's work was hardly subversive. His novel *The Cross and the Arrow* had been issued in a special edition of 140,000 copies by the U.S. Marine Corps. The film *Destination Tokyo*, for which he wrote the screenplay, was used by the military for training. *The House I Live In*, his short film about racial tolerance, was given an award by the Academy of Motion Picture Arts and Sciences. And one of his short stories, "The Happiest Man on Earth," was awarded first prize in the 1938 O. Henry Memorial Awards. Maltz once

Left: After being dismissed by the House Committee on Un-American Activities, Dalton Trumbo tries to get in the last word to scold Chairman J. Parnell Thomas. Trumbo's attorney, Robert W. Kenny, is on his right.

remarked that "writers . . . must be judged by their work and not by the committees they join." He maintained that if the HUAC found his work subversive, it wouldn't be long before they found other work they objected to in newspapers and magazines. "If it requires acceptance of the ideas of this committee to remain immune from the brand of un-Americanism," Maltz read, "then who is ultimately safe from this committee except members of the Ku Klux Klan?" His mention of the Ku Klux Klan (KKK), a white supremacist group that often resorted to violence to enforce its view of America, was a jab at the chairman and two other committee members, John S. Wood and John E. Rankin. All of these men were known to have strong ties to the KKK and were anti-Semitic as well. "I would rather die," Maltz testified, "than be a shabby American, groveling before men whose names are Thomas and Rankin, but who now carry out activities in America like those carried out in Germany. . . . The American people are going to have to choose between the Bill of Rights and the Thomas committee. They cannot have both."

Thomas rapped his gavel.

Stripling then repeatedly asked Maltz if he was a member of the Screen Writers Guild. When Maltz refused to answer the question directly, Stripling moved on to ask if the screenwriter was now or ever had been a member of the Communist Party. Again not satisfied with Maltz's response, Stripling pressed him. Maltz replied, "I have answered the question, Mr. Quisling." (A quisling is a traitor or collaborator.) The use of "Quisling" brought an objection from McDowell.

Thomas excused Maltz, but before he could step away from the stand, Stripling also called Attorney Robert W. Kenny to the stand so the committee could clarify an article that had appeared

Critics of the House Committee on Un-American Activities charged that it was a threat to the Constitution of the United States and the First Amendment and that it was un-American. Here J. Parnell Thomas seems to be suggesting to John E. Rankin that because the 1946 "Report of the President's Committee on Civil Rights" found constitutional violations in many facets of American life, the HUAC was on solid legal ground.

in the *Washington Times-Herald*. The article suggested that Kenny had advised the defense witnesses to refuse to answer the HUAC's two key questions. Kenny responded by reminding the committee that a lawyer's advice and communication with his clients are confidential and protected by law. Thomas knew it was useless to pursue the matter any further. After both Kenny and Maltz were dismissed, Thomas ordered Maltz's lengthy file of communist connections to be read into the record.

Alvah Bessie took the stand as the fourth unfriendly witness. Bessie had written the novel *Dwell in the Wilderness*, a family saga, and *Men in Battle*, about his service in the Abraham Lincoln Brigade during the Spanish Civil War. As a screenwriter for Warner Bros., Bessie also had written *The Very Thought of You*, *Objective Burma!*, and other scripts. He asked to read his prepared statement.

Thomas allowed the first couple of paragraphs and promised to put the statement into the record. Like the other witnesses before him, Bessie reminded the committee that it had no constitutional right to ask about the opinions or political beliefs of American citizens. "Now either the Constitution and its Bill of Rights mean what they say or they do not mean what they say," he said.

He warned that the real purpose of the HUAC hearings was to attack Roosevelt's New Dealers and their successors, adding that if the committee was allowed to continue its attack on the motion picture business, it would then go on "to the throttling of the press, the radio, the theater, and the book publishers of America." He reminded the committee that this was how Hitler had come to power in Germany.

After asking Bessie only a couple of questions about his

occupation and employment, Stripling asked him the committee's two most important questions. Bessie's answers fell along the same lines as those of the other three witnesses who had testified, and Thomas promptly excused him. His incriminating file, which included a Communist Party membership card and seven pages listing thirty-two separate Communist affiliations, was read into the record. The offenses were by now familiar: writing articles for various Communist Party publications, appearing on a program with known communists, sponsoring organizations the committee considered to be communist fronts, and supporting and fighting in the Spanish Civil War. These charges prompted Thomas to comment, "I don't think this committee has ever looked into anything where we have found more evidence of Communist activities than we have found in Hollywood."

By now, the HUAC had fallen into a routine. One of the unfriendly witnesses would be called to testify and sworn in, a witness statement would usually be passed to Thomas to consider if it was relevant to the inquiry, and a decision would be rendered—a denial more often than not.

The next screenwriter took the stand on Wednesday, October 29. Samuel Ornitz was known for co-writing the script for the 1938 movie *Little Orphan Annie*, based on a popular comic strip by Harold Gray. When he passed his statement to the gentlemen on the stage, McDowell dismissed it, saying, "I wouldn't have any part of it."

Stripling asked the committee's questions: Are you a member of the Screen Writers Guild? Are you now or have you ever been a member of the Communist Party?

In responding, Ornitz said the answers involved "a serious question of conscience" and accused the chairman of "practicing

71

intimidation." Like those who had taken the stand earlier, he was attempting to answer by casting accusations at the committee and avoiding the simple responses that Thomas demanded.

With a flourish of his gavel, Thomas proclaimed, "The witness is through. . . . Stand away."

At least the sixth unfriendly witness, screenwriter Herbert Biberman, provided a bit of variety when he responded to Stripling's question about his birth. "I was born within a stone's throw of Independence Hall in Philadelphia, on the day [not year] when Mr. McKinley was inaugurated as President of the United States, March 4, 1900, on the second floor of a building at Sixth and South, over a grocery store." Stripling hoped that all of Biberman's

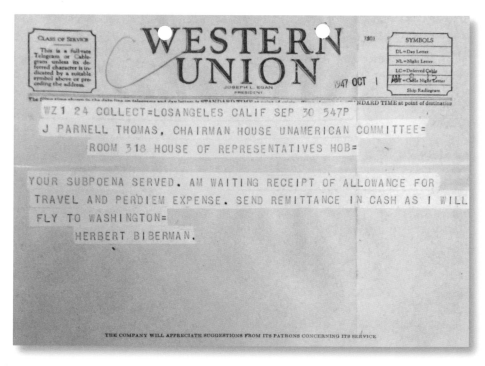

On September 30, 1947, Herbert Biberman informed Chairman
J. Parnell Thomas that he was waiting for a travel allowance, "in cash," because he planned to fly to Washington, DC, to make his appearance before the House Committee on Un-American Activities.

responses would be as detailed and specific. This, however, was not to be. Biberman's written statement was rejected by Thomas as "another case of vilification." His responses to Stripling's $32 and $64 questions also did not pass muster with Thomas, who banged his gavel incessantly. Finally, Biberman addressed Thomas directly, saying, "Mr. Chairman, I would be very suspicious of any answer that came out of my mouth that pleased this committee."

Still exercising his gavel, Thomas ordered, "Take him away." The order was delivered like a judge speaking to a bailiff or a king to an executioner.

According to Gordon Kahn, Edward Dmytryk and producer Adrian Scott had been subpoenaed because of their film *Crossfire*,

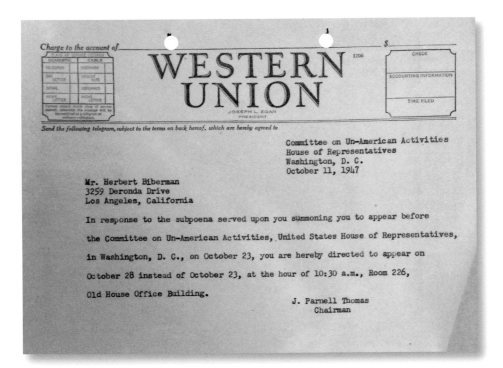

A Western Union telegram informing Herbert Biberman of a change in the order in which witnesses would testify before the House Committee on Un-American Activities.

which "attacked anti-Semitism in particular and racial hatred and intolerance generally." Dmytryk wrote in his memoir that the film was "the first to use the word *Jew* openly (and pejoratively [in a negative way], when used by the murderer)." That the film's director and producer were summoned to appear before the HUAC was fitting, given that the committee had long stood accused of being anti-Semitic and racially biased. When Dmytryk asked to read his statement, Thomas dismissed it, saying it was "typical of the other statements that we have inspected." Stripling jumped straight to the two questions burning in the minds of the committee members, and when Dmytryk didn't offer them the answers they wanted, he was excused.

Witnesses who weren't allowed to read their statements during the hearings released them to the newspapers. In Dmytryk's statement, he accused the committee of demanding "that the producers 'clean their own house,' under the supervision of the Committee's members. They will name the names and the producers must make out the blacklist. But where will it all end?"

Adrian Scott was next. As Thomas read Scott's statement to himself, his face grew more crimson by the second. As Kahn witnessed, it "caused the Chairman almost to blow a gasket." Thomas remarked, "This may not be the worst statement we have received, but it is almost the worst. . . . Therefore, it is clearly out of order, not pertinent at all, hasn't anything to do with the inquiry, and the Chair will rule that the statement will not be read." What Scott had written showed his contempt for the HUAC: "Today this committee is engaged in an attempt to destroy nineteen subpoenaed witnesses. The record of these men is clear. They have always stood for issues which are beneficial to the great mass of the American people."

Scott was excused from the witness stand. One of the committee's investigators then read aloud their files on Scott and Dmytryk, and these were placed into the record.

In Kahn's view, on Thursday Thomas arrived "at the hearing room looking like a man with a delicious secret." Perhaps it was the change in tactics he planned to try with Ring Lardner Jr., the ninth of the nineteen witnesses. In 1943, Lardner had won an Oscar for co-writing the screenplay for *Woman of the Year*, starring Katharine Hepburn as a progressive journalist and Spencer Tracy as her more traditional sportswriter husband. Based on that triumph and a new contract from Twentieth Century–Fox film studio, Lardner and his wife had bought a new home during the summer of 1947, just before his "subpoena from Mr. Thomas was delivered in September." The chairman allowed that the screenwriter would be able to read his statement *after* his testimony.

Unfortunately for Thomas, Lardner was as reluctant to offer the committee yes or no answers as the others had been. To the question about the Screen Writers Guild, Lardner replied, "I want to be cooperative about this, but there are certain limits to my cooperation. I don't want to help you divide or smash this particular guild, or to infiltrate the motion-picture business in any way for the purpose which seems to me to be to try to control that business, to control what the American people can see and hear in their motion-picture theaters."

"Now, Mr. Lardner," Thomas cautioned, "don't do like the others . . . or you will never read your statement."

But Lardner *was* like the others. He refused to give Thomas and the committee what they wanted. For a morning that began with Thomas in a cordial mood, things turned sour fast.

Actor Larry Parks (left) points to where Ring Lardner Jr. (center) should sign his name on a petition to abolish the House Committee on Un-American Activities. Actor and writer Waldo Salt, who eventually would be blacklisted, is on the right.

Lardner repeatedly refused to answer their questions directly. Thomas, furious at him for not cooperating, shouted three times, "Leave the witness chair."

Standing, Lardner leaned in to the microphone and half-joked, "I think I am leaving by force."

Thomas was seething now. "Sergeant, take the witness away," he ordered.

As with the other witnesses, the allegations of pro-communist activity against Lardner were read into the record. They were recorded by the news reporters and newsreel cameras under the glaring lights in the Caucus Room.

Thomas's change of mood didn't bode well for screenwriter Lester Cole. Almost as soon as Cole took the stand and identified himself, Thomas asked if he was a member of the Screen Writers Guild. "Mr. Chairman," Cole replied, "I would like at this time to make a statement."

Cole wrote in his 1981 autobiography that before he went east to the HUAC hearings, Louis B. Mayer, head of Metro-Goldwyn-Mayer Studios (MGM), had urged him to break with the "commies that you're tied up with." Whether fact or shaded by time, Cole maintained that Mayer offered to double his salary if he would renounce his membership in the Communist Party.

Shaking his head, Cole responded to Mayer, "You're a very generous man. I wish I could go along with you, but I can't." For Cole, it was all about principle. It was about the government peering into people's lives and asking questions he felt it had no right to ask. It was true, too, that Cole had not been blinded by his own success as a writer. When he looked around and saw the poverty and hunger that existed in the world's richest nation, he thought there must be a better way, one that didn't advocate equality

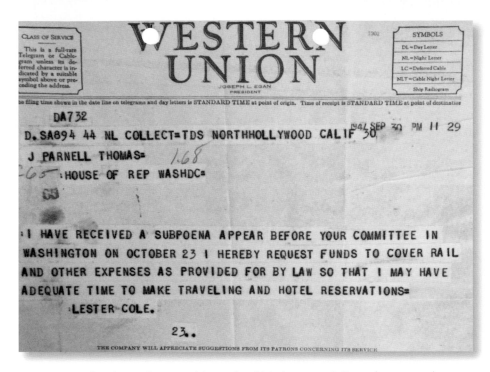

CLASS OF SERVICE

This is a full-rate Telegram or Cablegram unless its deferred character is indicated by a suitable symbol above or preceding the address.

WESTERN UNION

JOSEPH L. EGAN
PRESIDENT

SYMBOLS

DL = Day Letter

NL = Night Letter

LC = Deferred Cable

NLT = Cable Night Letter

Ship Radiogram

be filing time shown in the date line on telegrams and day letters is STANDARD TIME at point of origin. Time of receipt is STANDARD TIME at point of destination

DA732

D. SA894 44 NL COLLECT=TDS NORTHHOLLYWOOD CALIF 30 1947 SEP 30 PM 11 29

J PARNELL THOMAS= *1.68*

65 : HOUSE OF REP WASHDC=

:I HAVE RECEIVED A SUBPOENA APPEAR BEFORE YOUR COMMITTEE IN
WASHINGTON ON OCTOBER 23 I HEREBY REQUEST FUNDS TO COVER RAIL
AND OTHER EXPENSES AS PROVIDED FOR BY LAW SO THAT I MAY HAVE
ADEQUATE TIME TO MAKE TRAVELING AND HOTEL RESERVATIONS=

:LESTER COLE.

23.

THE COMPANY WILL APPRECIATE SUGGESTIONS FROM ITS PATRONS CONCERNING ITS SERVICE

Lester Cole planned to travel by rail to Washington, DC, and requested funds to do so. Ultimately, those summoned to appear before the House Committee on Un-American Activities had to pay for their own travel expenses.

in the nation's historic documents only but that actually lived up to that promise.

Now, before the committee, Cole handed a copy of his statement up to the members on the stage.

Cole later described what happened: "My turn came. Unfriendly Witness number ten. Having seen all but one of the statements offered rejected after the first two sentences were read, as 'Vilifying, subversive,' the previous night I revised my opening paragraph to make it milder, but equally truthful. It read: 'I want to say at the outset that I am a loyal American, who upholds the Constitution and Bill of Rights of my country, who does not advocate force and violence or subversion, and who is not an agent of a foreign power.' Thomas hardly glanced at it, certainly not for enough time to read it. He tossed it aside and said, 'Like the others. Vilification, subversive. Request denied.'"

Cole attempted to ask a couple of questions of the chairman, but Thomas cut him off. "You will not ask anything," Thomas told him, and he ordered Stripling to proceed.

In answer to the question about the Screen Writers Guild, Cole attempted to explain why he thought it was being asked. This did not sit well with Thomas. As Cole recalled, "The little fat man got red in the face, banged his gavel fourteen times, shouting, 'No!' with each bang."

"It is a very simple question," Thomas explained.

"It isn't necessarily that simple," Cole said.

Thomas inquired, "Are you able to answer the question 'Yes' or 'No,' or are you unable to answer it 'Yes' or 'No'?"

Cole responded, "I am not able to answer 'Yes' or 'No.' I am able, and I would like to answer it in my own way."

"First," Thomas said, "we want you to answer 'Yes' or 'No,' then you can make some explanation of your answer."

Like the others, Cole was dismissed, and one of the committee's investigators ticked off the items in his file.

The committee expected a victory with the eleventh witness, Bertolt Brecht. "It was just before noon," Gordon Kahn wrote. "The tempo of the Committee was being speeded up to match the hectic rhythm pounded out by Chairman Thomas' gavel. Everything, this Thursday morning, had to be quickly out and rapidly dried, for Mr. Thomas had promised a world-shaking revelation, and the world did not want to wait."

Brecht was a German-born playwright and poet whose command of the English language was limited. The committee provided him with an interpreter from the Library of Congress, but Thomas had more trouble understanding the interpreter than he did Brecht. Whether Brecht understood that Thomas had ruled against his statement being read is not clear, but he launched into reading it anyway. He told the committee about how he'd had to leave his homeland in 1933, when Hitler came to power, because much of his work was anti-Nazi. He first went to Denmark but had to leave when Hitler invaded that country. From Denmark, he traveled to Sweden, and then eventually to Finland, where he awaited his visa to the United States. He arrived in the U.S. in 1941. His connection to Hollywood was through a story he'd sold to an independent producer. That story, *Hangmen Also Die*, was turned into a screenplay, but Brecht did not write it. He was not a screenwriter. Given this information, it was pointless for Stripling to ask if he was a member of the Screen Writers Guild, so Stripling cut to the chase, asking, "Are you now or have you ever been a member of the Communist Party of any country?"

Unlike the other witnesses, Brecht was forthcoming with his answers. "I am a guest in this country and do not want to enter into any legal arguments," he said, "so I will answer your question fully as well [as] I can. I was not a member or am not a member of any Communist Party."

Stripling continued, "Mr. Brecht, is it true that you have written a number of very revolutionary poems, plays, and other writings?"

"I have written a number of poems and songs and plays in the fight against Hitler and, of course, they can be considered, therefore, as revolutionary because I . . . was for the overthrow of that government."

Thomas wanted to speed things along. "We are not interested

Berthold (Bertolt) Brecht told the committee that he was not and never had been a member of any Communist Party, but he was well schooled in communist philosophy.

in any works that he might have written advocating the over-throw of Germany or the government there," he told Stripling.

Stripling pointed out that "from an examination of the works which Mr. Brecht has written . . . he seems to be a person of international importance to the Communist revolutionary movement." He quoted the investigators' translations of Brecht's work as evidence against Brecht. The only problem was that he misquoted them, and Brecht had to explain their meaning.

At one point, Stripling interrupted Brecht to ask if his writings were "pro-Communist or anti-Communist, or would . . . take a neutral position regarding Communists."

Brecht answered by saying that "literature has the right and the duty to give to the public the ideas of the time."

Brecht was proving to be more difficult than the committee had thought. Stripling changed course and asked, "Have you ever made application to join the Communist Party?"

Brecht was quick to answer, "No, no, no, no, no, never."

An unread portion of Brecht's statement applied directly to the charges frequently made against the committee. It read, "Being called before the Un-American Activities Committee, . . . I feel free for the first time to say a few words about American matters: looking back at my experiences as a playwright and a poet in the Europe of the last two decades, I wish to say that the great American people would lose much and risk much if they allowed anybody to restrict free competition of ideas in cultural fields, or to interfere with art which must be free in order to be art."

Brecht was excused, but not before Thomas commented, "You are a good example to the witnesses of Mr. Kenny and Mr. Crum."

Cole, who shared a taxi ride back to their hotel with Brecht later that day, recalled that "Brecht grieved; he wondered whether any of us would ever understand and forgive him [for answering the committee's questions]. Alone in this country, a foreigner, they could hold him . . . in prison for how long—? He wanted to go home, to the new German Democratic Republic, where there was work for him to do. I put an arm around him. Little comfort. At the hotel he explained. The others did understand. And the next morning, early, he bid us farewell. Within a day he was on a ship for Europe."

That afternoon, at two o'clock, Thomas once again presented Louis J. Russell. The former FBI agent had been on the stand many times during the week to read the files of the unfriendly witnesses. This was his eleventh appearance. Those in the Caucus Room assumed he was just the warm-up act for Thomas's surprise revelation. But it turned out that he held the surprise. Stripling asked, "Mr. Russell, can you tell the committee whether or not the Soviet Government has ever sent an official representative to the motion-picture industry?"

Russell told the committee about a cultural exchange between Russia and the U.S., but he didn't offer any evidence of subversion. Perhaps his most shocking revelation was "that Soviet spies tried unsuccessfully to buy U.S. atomic secrets as early as November, 1942, 33 months before the first atomic bomb was exploded." He failed, however, to make any connection between those alleged attempts and any of "the Hollywood personalities who figured in the hearings." Although a few newspaper headlines shouted about a connection between Hollywood, the HUAC hearings, and the attempt to purchase plans for the A-bomb, the only connection seemed to be that the information had been revealed at the hearings. Thomas's surprise turned out to be somewhat of a dud.

What did stun everyone, though, was Thomas's sudden and unexpected announcement after Russell left the witness stand: "The hearings today conclude the first phase of the committee's investigation of communism in the motion-picture industry." The hearings were supposed to have lasted three weeks, but after nine days of testimony, the chairman adjourned them on Thursday, October 30, with one parting bit of advice: "The industry should set about immediately to clean its own house and not wait for public opinion to force it to do so."

For now, the hearings were over. A month earlier, nineteen men had been summoned to Washington, DC, to testify before the House Committee on Un-American Activities. These nineteen had been labeled by the *Hollywood Reporter* as "unfriendly." At the end of October, ten of the nineteen witnesses, who all believed that the Constitution and its First Amendment guaranteed them freedom of association and freedom of thought, became known as the Hollywood Ten. They were Albert Maltz, Dalton Trumbo, Adrian Scott, Samuel Ornitz, John Howard Lawson, Edward Dmytryk, Lester Cole, Herbert Biberman, Alvah Bessie, and Ring Lardner Jr.

The fate of these men now lay in the hands of the entire House of Representatives. The committee had unanimously recommended that all of them be cited for contempt of Congress for not answering to the government's satisfaction the questions about membership in the Screen Writers Guild or Communist Party. If a majority of the House agreed, the cases would be sent to federal court with a recommendation that the men be tried and punished. The punishment for contempt of Congress, if they were found guilty, was up to one year in prison and a $1,000 fine.

At the conclusion of the hearings, a jovial J. Parnell Thomas (right) tells reporters that the House of Representatives will be asked to vote on contempt charges brought against the Hollywood Ten.

VERDICT

On Monday, November 24, 1947, the Committee on Un-American Activities presented its case against the Hollywood Ten to the full House of Representatives. The committee started with Albert Maltz, offering a select portion of his testimony—including the part where Maltz referred to Robert E. Stripling as Mr. Quisling.

Chairman J. Parnell Thomas told the members of Congress about the "extensive campaign launched in the United States to vilify" the HUAC and "to confuse the American people into believing that in asking these witnesses to state whether or not they were members of the Communist Party," the committee was invading their constitutional rights. He added that treating the Communist Party as equivalent to the Republican and Democratic Parties would be a grave mistake. He asked the full body to cite Maltz for contempt.

When Thomas finished, committee member Richard B. Vail, a Republican from Illinois, picked up the drumbeat. Though mostly silent during the hearings, he dismissed the unfriendly witnesses as nothing more than dangerous dupes of communism. He painted the Communist Party USA as a tool of a foreign system bent on overthrowing the U.S. government.

Herman P. Eberharter, a Democrat from Pennsylvania, was allowed a few minutes to speak. He was not a member of the HUAC, and his comments may have surprised and disheartened Thomas. Eberharter asked, "Should a committee of this House expect the support of Members of this body when it flies in the face of constitutional guarantees . . . ?" Gordon Kahn suggested that Eberharter may have sensed the committee's desire to dictate the content of Hollywood's movies. However, the congressman believed the American people were capable of censoring Hollywood themselves by either purchasing movie tickets or not. He reminded the HUAC that it had been asked again and again for the list of films it reportedly had that were subversive. The committee had never supplied the list. He finished by telling Congress, "We can support the recommendations of the Committee on Un-American Activities for citations for contempt of Congress, or we can support free speech. We cannot have both. . . . If Americanism means anything, it means that no group of persons, however exalted, can dictate what is, or is not, Americanism."

In the end, the House of Representatives voted 346 to 17 to approve the citation against Maltz for contempt of Congress. Maltz had been the committee's test case, the one most probable to sway Congress to uphold the HUAC's recommendation, because he was "arrogant," according to Robert McDowell.

Dalton Trumbo's fate was decided next in a vote of 240 to 15 to follow the HUAC's advice. Before Trumbo's contempt of Congress citation came down, Karl E. Mundt had a chance to speak. Although Mundt was a member of the HUAC, he had not attended any of its hearings. He had, however, conferred with leading members of the movie industry, and he reported that it was poised to blacklist communists and anyone else who failed to respond to the committee's questions. He read a resolution from Twentieth Century–Fox, which said the studio would "dispense with the services of any employe who is an acknowledged Communist or of any employe who refuses to answer a question . . . by any committee of the Congress of the United States and is cited for contempt." He added that he was supporting a bill before Congress to increase the fine for contempt from $1,000 to $5,000 and the time in prison from one year to five years.

"The remaining eight cases were handled in rapid-fire order without debate and by voice vote," according to the *New York Times*. Enjoying the victory, Thomas declared, "The Constitution was never intended to cloak or shield those who would destroy it." He insisted that the citations were the result of the witnesses' refusal to cooperate and answer the committee's questions, but he also admitted that they had not been chosen at random. They had been subpoenaed and presented one after the other "because our investigation had disclosed that they were Communists or had long records of Communist affiliation and activities."

Not everyone agreed that the Hollywood Ten should be charged with contempt of Congress. About the HUAC's procedures and findings, California representative Helen Gahagan Douglas, a former actress and the wife of actor Melvyn Douglas, said, "The Hollywood hearings were a tragic farce."

All that remained now was the prosecution of the unfriendly ten. Tom C. Clark, the U.S. attorney general, asked George Morris Fay, the U.S. attorney for the District of Columbia, to

Hollywood GENERAL.

AMERICANS FOR DEMOCRATIC ACTION

1740 K Street, N. W., Washington 6, D. C., EXecutive 8160

October 14, 1947

Rep. J. Parnell Thomas
Chairman, Committee on Un-American Activities
House Office Building
Washington, D. C.

Dear Mr. Thomas:

Cultural freedom is one of the great and enduring
pillars of American democracy. It is one of the freedoms
that most dramatically differentiates our society
from totalitarian regimes where creative artists are
compelled to wear uniforms and march the goosestep.
A democratic system does not fear ideas. It believes
that in the competition of ideas men will most readily
find truth.

Because this freedom is so basic and meaningful,
Americans for Democratic Action views with deep concern any move that narrows the realm of cultrual
liberty and imprisons the imagination of writers and
artists. Opposing Communists no less vehemently than
we resist Fascism, we are determined to combat with
equal passion any attempt to impose the kind of mental
straight-jacket which stifles culture under dictator-
ship.

Democracy has historically tried to stimulate and
enlarge the imagination of creative workers, in the
belief that no horizon is too wide and no thought
too "dangerous" for a people devoted to freedom.
There is no question of the fundamental devotion of
Americans to their democratic institutions. That is
as true in Hollywood as it is anywhere else.

It is undoubtedly true that some Communists have
sought to make their influence felt in Hollywood --
as everywhere else. The greatest service we can
render to them is to discredit a whole community and
a whole area of our creative life because some Communists may have found their way into it.

Leon Henderson, an economist and key aide to President Franklin D.
Roosevelt, and actor Melvyn Douglas, of Americans for Democratic Action
(ADA), were fearful that the Thomas Committee was attempting to censor
or dictate the content of movies and wrote to the chairman to express their
concerns. The ADA was one of many liberal organizations dedicated to
protecting the freedoms guaranteed by the Constitution. (Letter continues
on page 92.)

Reckless attacks on liberals committed by the House Committee on Un-American Affairs in the past have repeatedly strengthened the hand of Communist agents. They have used such attacks to prove that our democracy is a frail and frightened thing and to proclaim that legitimate exposure of their activities must inevitably degenerate into a ruthless heresy hunt. The Communists will undoubtedly attempt to raise the same cry in connection with the hearings which you are conducting this month.

We believe the movies -- like the press and radio -- need more freedom, not less, more daring and initiative, not greater timidity and conformism.

We do not want monolithic movies, whether the scenario is dictated by a totalitarian bureaucrat or a Congressional Committee.

We believe that the hearings will inevitably create an atmosphere which inpairs originality and ingenuity.

Since your Committee, however, is apparently determined to conduct the hearings, we ask positive steps to avert a repetition of past injustices and to eliminate the repressive aspect of the investigation.

We urge revision of Committee procedure to permit those whose names may be freely assaulted to appear in their own defense, accompanied by counsel, and to cross examine their accusers.

Without these basic legal safeguards, your investigations can only encourage suppression of democratic dissent and strengthen the very forces you purport to expose.

Sincerely yours,

Leon Henderson

Leon Henderson
Chairman, Executive Committee

Melvyn Douglas

Melvyn Douglas
Chairman, California ADA
Organizing Committee

The second page of the letter from Leon Henderson and Melvyn Douglas.

bring the men to trial because "the authority of the Congress must be maintained."

Early the next morning, most of the Hollywood Ten took the train back to Los Angeles. There was work to be done. They had to assure their wives and children that despite the contempt citations, everything would be fine. They also needed to raise money to pay their lawyers and, should things not end well in federal court, mount an appeal. If necessary, they would go all the way to the U.S. Supreme Court. The Court, their lawyers assured them, was weighted with liberal-minded justices who would support their First Amendment argument. The men also purchased newspaper space to explain to the public what they were doing, declaring that "every free institution in America is jeopardized as long as this committee exists."

Almost immediately, they set off on cross-country speaking tours. Most sold their homes to provide money for their defense and to support their families in the event they were convicted and sentenced to prison. Some even tried to secure personal loans. But selling their homes and qualifying for loans proved difficult. Trumbo reported that no banks would lend them money and that selling their property had to be done quickly and quietly before word of their desperation got out and opportunists descended.

Five days before Thomas asked the full House to vote contempt citations on the Hollywood Ten, Eric Johnston went before cameras in New York City. A month earlier, he had assured the nineteen subpoenaed men that he and the Motion Picture Association of America would never impose a blacklist. According to Lester Cole, however, Johnston "had privately agreed with Thomas that a blacklist *should* exist." He had pushed the idea on behalf of Thomas with studio executives,

Michael Cole (right), Nikola Trumbo, and an unidentified youth count money raised for the defense of their fathers, all members of the Hollywood Ten.

TONIGHT
"KEEP AMERICA FREE"
RALLY

For the 19 Hollywood Progressives
Subpoenaed by Thomas-Rankin

MEET THEM ALL!

Alvah BESSIE • Herbert BIBERMAN • Berchtold BRECHT • Lester COLE • Richard COLLINS • Edward DMYTRYK • Gordon KAHN • Howard KOCH • Ring LARDNER, Jr. • John Howard LAWSON • Albert MALTZ • Lewis MILESTONE • Samuel ORNITZ • Larry PARKS • Irving PICHEL • Robert ROSSEN • Waldo SALT • Adrian SCOTT • Dalton TRUMBO.

HEAR THESE LEADING LIBERALS!
Senator Claude PEPPER

Bartley CRUM   **Robert KENNY**
(Attorneys for the 19)

John GARFIELD   **Paul DRAPER**
Lillian HELLMAN   **Frank KINGDON**
Dr. Harlow SHAPLEY

See Larry Parks, Irving Pichel and others in Dramatic Presentation of the Un-American Committee in Action!

ST. NICHOLAS ARENA
69 West 66th Street, N. Y. C.   8:00 P. M.
TICKETS: 60c—$1.20—$1.80

Tickets on Sale: St. Nicholas Arena Box Office; PCA Office, 205 E. 42nd St. MU 3-5580; Bookfair, 133 W. 44th St., N.Y.C.

Sponsored by **PROGRESSIVE CITIZENS OF AMERICA**

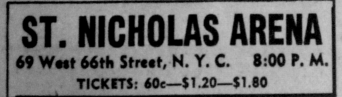 **ATTEND THE NATIONAL CONFERENCE ON CULTURAL FREEDOM AND CIVIL LIBERTIES**

Hotel Commodore, Oct. 25-26. Hear America's leading artists, scientists and professional men speak up against threats to freedom.

who turned it down as legally too risky. Now, in what became known as the Waldorf Statement, Johnston called for "a national policy to govern the employment of Communists in private industry." Without legislation to guide studio executives, he said, they themselves "must . . . take positive steps to meet this problem and do so promptly." The first of those steps had been to call the top Hollywood brass to New York's Waldorf Astoria hotel for closed-door talks. The second, after the talks concluded, was to "discharge or suspend without compensation those [men] in our employ, and we will not re-employ any of the ten until such time as he is acquitted or has purged himself of contempt and declares under oath that he is not a Communist."

Despite having contracts with Scott, Dmytryk, Cole, Lardner, and Trumbo, the studios "suspended" these men. This meant the studios paid them no salaries. Lawson, Maltz, Bessie, Ornitz, and Biberman were blacklisted immediately. All their names were circulated throughout the industry, making the ten unemployable. These actions encouraged newspaper owner William Randolph Hearst to call for federal censorship of motion pictures. Johnston, his loyalty lying with his employers, felt the need to warn the public of the potential danger if the legislature listened to Hearst. "If the motion picture is to be censored," he said, "then the newspapers must be too; and the books; and the magazines, and the radio." Critics of the HUAC maintained that by dismissing the ten and

Left: Before and after they were summoned to Washington, DC, to appear before the House Committee on Un-American Activities, the nineteen unfriendly witnesses and some of their supporters gave talks around the country to inform the public about how the committee was trampling on the Constitution and to earn money for their defense. Shown here is an advertisement for an event planned in New York City.

Five screenwriters suspended without pay after the release of the Waldorf Statement get together to draft a response to movie heads on November 25, 1947. They are, from left, Herbert Biberman, Samuel Ornitz (standing), Adrian Scott, Edward Dmytryk, and John Howard Lawson.

blacklisting them from employment, the industry had already caved in to those seeking to control the content of movies.

Why did powerful men such as MGM's Louis B. Mayer, Harry Cohn of Columbia Pictures, Albert Warner of Warner Bros., Dore Schary of Radio-Keith-Orpheum Pictures (RKO Radio Pictures), and some forty-four others rush to New York at Johnston's insistence? Filmland's reputation for producing family-friendly motion pictures had been badly damaged by the hearings. Ed Sullivan, a gossip columnist for the *New York Daily News*, suggested that the studio chiefs had little choice. Wall Street financiers, who were the real bosses of Hollywood, were concerned about their investments and demanded that something be done.

That sentiment was echoed by *New York Times* film critic Bosley Crowther, who wrote, "It should be fully realized that this action [the blacklist] was engineered by the major New York executives, the industry's overlords, and not by the 'Hollywood producers.'" The studio men were mostly interested in saving their positions, for which they were paid handsomely. Mayer publicly boasted that he earned $1 million per year, making him the highest-paid executive in America at the time. It was also the opinion of many both inside and outside Hollywood that an agreement had been reached between the HUAC and studio investors that further investigations of the movie industry would be called off if a blacklist was put into effect.

Within days of the announced suspensions and blacklist, Hollywood guilds began to adopt anti-communist policies. While the Hollywood Ten still had their supporters, some members of the Committee for the First Amendment who had flown to

Washington in October to support them now feared being caught up in the hysteria. Membership in the progressive group began to evaporate almost overnight. Hollywood star Humphrey Bogart was one of those who worried that his support of the ten might be misread by his fans and, more important, by the studio bosses who signed his paychecks. He bought space for a full-page magazine ad that read in part, "My recent trip to Washington, where I appeared with a group of motion picture people, has become the subject of such confused and erroneous interpretations that I feel the situation should be clarified. I am not a Communist. I am not a Communist sympathizer. I detest Communism just as any other decent American does. . . . That the trip was ill-advised, even foolish, I am very ready to admit. At the time it seemed the thing to do."

The powerful entertainment reporter Hedda Hopper condemned the Hollywood Ten and some of the films they and others had written. She was convinced that communist writers routinely slipped Red propaganda into movies without the knowledge of the actors or studio executives. She named two pictures which, in her view, worked to destroy the faith of Americans in their government and in the free enterprise system. *Mr. Smith Goes to Washington* (1939), as Hopper saw it, left the impression "that there were only two honest men among the 96 members of the Senate of the United States." *The Farmer's Daughter* (1947), an amusing comedy, held "up to ridicule our whole process of free elections, by showing a crowd of Americans madly applauding gibberish and double talk at a political rally." Films that seemed to question American politics were, in her opinion, subject to the charge of being un-American.

At the same time, she made allowances for other movies the HUAC had targeted as communistic. Three pictures—*Mission to Moscow*, *The North Star*, and *Song of Russia*—showed a prosperous USSR instead of one filled with discord and food shortages, which was the reality of Russia in 1947. But they had been made during World War II, when the USSR was an ally and "at a time when everyone hoped we could understand Russia." She accepted the necessity to shine a favorable light on the country given the time in which the movies were made and the U.S. relationship with Russia during the war.

Meanwhile, Hopper's mail reflected the thoughts of her readers nationwide. Singer Bing Crosby's sister-in-law wrote to say, "My blood boiled to hear such men as Lawson, stand up and yell at the investigating committee, practically idiotic with hysteria." Another reader observed that in casting Lauren Bacall in the upcoming movie version of Ayn Rand's *The Fountainhead*, Warner Bros. was "ignoring the feelings of the AMERICAN theater-going public. . . . I am sure the box office receipts will manifest our views, more emphatically than words." Not satisfied with airing her distaste for Bacall, now branded a communist or, at the very least, a sympathizer for her support of the nineteen, the reader went on to attack Bacall's husband, Humphrey Bogart: "This is applicable also to Bogart." (Bacall eventually dropped out of the film and was replaced by actress Patricia Neal.) Members of the Committee for the First Amendment, including Bacall and Bogart, were scrambling to cut their ties with the Hollywood Ten in order to save their reputations and careers. Bacall now claimed she and her husband had been hoodwinked into showing their support.

The Hollywood Ten soon realized that defending themselves

wasn't going to come cheaply. After conferring with their lawyers and the federal prosecutor, they agreed to accept the verdicts against John Howard Lawson and Dalton Trumbo as verdicts for all. Whatever decisions were reached in the cases against these two men would apply to them all, without eight more individual trials going before a judge and jury. Their attorneys felt it would be difficult to find a sympathetic jury in Washington, DC, where almost everyone worked in one way or another for the government. They assured the men that the final verdict would be decided on appeal, all the way up to the liberal-leaning Supreme Court if necessary.

The first to be tried for contempt of Congress was Lawson. On April 19, 1948, after two hours and fifteen minutes, the jury returned its verdict: guilty of contempt of Congress for refusing to answer the HUAC's questions. Trumbo's trial came a little over two weeks later. On May 5, after two hours of deliberation, the jury of seven men and five women found him guilty as well. Trumbo's attorney, Charles Houston, argued that his client "was in the process of answering all the time. The refusal was not from Dalton Trumbo, but from the committee," when it abruptly excused him from the witness stand. Both men would face sentencing at a later date.

Since the guilty verdicts for Lawson and Trumbo applied to all the men, they tried to write as much as possible—working "in the early morning and late at night"—before Lawson's and Trumbo's appeals were heard. Because all were now blacklisted, some of the writers submitted their work under pseudonyms. "In a few weeks, it became possible for a producer to buy a first-class script at a fire-sale price," Dmytryk wrote in his memoir.

FEDERAL BUREAU OF INVESTIGATION

Form No. 1
THIS CASE ORIGINATED AT LOS ANGELES   FILE NO. 46-1844

REPORT MADE AT	DATE WHEN MADE	PERIOD FOR WHICH MADE	REPORT MADE BY
LOS ANGELES	11/16/49	9/21-23,26-30 10/3-5,19/49	

TITLE
LESTER COLE, was. Lester Le Roy Cole,
Lester Cohen, J. Redmond Prior

CHARACTER OF CASE
FRAUD AGAINST THE GOVERNMENT

SYNOPSIS OF FACTS:

Warner Brothers Studios paid $20,000 on March 1, 1948
for an original story, "These Many Years," written by
J. REDMOND PRIOR, in deal negotiated by NAT GOLLSTONE
AGENCY. PRIOR allegedly pseudonym for LESTER COLE,
one of the "unfriendly 10" Hollywood witnesses indicted
for contempt of Congress.

(7)(D)

deny knowledge of PRIOR's
identity — were told name was a pseudonym for a New
York author. LESTER COLE and wife, JEANNE, admitted
to T-9 that he sold a story to Warner Brothers in
1948 for $20,000 through NAT GOLLSTONE AGENCY.

- C -

DETAILS: 5 ENCLS FILED WITH ORIG.

AT LOS ANGELES, CALIFORNIA:

ALL INFORMATION CONTAINED
HEREIN IS UNCLASSIFIED
DATE 3/2/79 BY 2333

This is a joint report and investigation of SA
and the writer.

APPROVED AND FORWARDED:	SPECIAL AGENT IN CHARGE	DO NOT WRITE IN THESE SPACES	
COPIES OF THIS REPORT		100 2230	SE 22
5-Bureau (Encs.) 2-Los Angeles		NOT RECORDED 98 DEC 20 1949	INITIALS ON ORIGINAL

U. S. GOVERNMENT PRINTING OFFICE   7—2034

The FBI investigation turned up a payment from Warner Bros. to
J. Redmond Prior, which an anonymous informant suggested was a
pseudonym used by Lester Cole. FBI director J. Edgar Hoover told the
HUAC that the name likely belonged to one of the Hollywood Ten
because of the "Red" in "Redmond."

Cole submitted a movie script to Warner Bros. under the name J. Redmond Prior, his wife's maiden name. The studio bought it for $20,000, thinking it would be a good film for Humphrey Bogart. But Cole discovered that writing under a false name wasn't as easy as it seemed. Jack Warner wanted to meet this new talent. When an unidentified informant pointed to Cole as the writer, Warner was willing "to disguise [Cole's] connection with the film once the story leaked to the press." Alerted to what was going on, the FBI got involved. According to Cole's FBI file, "The informant said that, in his opinion, if COLE actually is the author, the plan might be for the story [movie] to come out, be accepted by the public without knowledge of the author's identity, and then COLE and the 'Hollywood 10' could point this out as an example that the merit of a story is what it states and not the politics of the author." Cole wrote, "If they couldn't prosecute for subversion, they might at least charge me with fraud," or failure to report the $20,000 on his income tax return. Indeed, the FBI was interested in seeing Cole's tax return for that year: "SUGGEST BUREAU DETERMINE WHETHER COLE-S FORTYEIGHT [sic] INCOME TAX RETURN SHOWS . . . TWENTY THOUSAND DOLLAR PAYMENT." The investigator must have been disappointed when he discovered that Cole not only had claimed the income but also paid the taxes due on it.

Most of the Hollywood Ten were also crisscrossing the country giving speeches. Once again, the FBI monitored everything they did and said, noting what groups they spoke to and who was in the audience. License plate numbers were recorded, as well as addresses the men visited and when they arrived and left. Notations were made as to who else was present, and the information was sent to Washington. The men were also

WASH FROM LOS ANGELES 6   28   8-01 PM

DIRECTOR   ATTN. MR. LADD.   URGENT

LESTER COLE, WA, FAG. REMYTEL SEPT. TWENTYSEVEN LAST

███████████████████ STATES COLE NOT EMPLOYED BY THEIR STUDIO

SINCE NINETEEN FORTYFOUR AND NOT EMPLOYED BY THEM NOW. IN MARCH

NINETEEEN FORTYEIGHT WARNER BROS BOUGHT AN ORIGINAL UNPUBLISHED

STORY OFFERED BY NAT GOLDSTONE AGENCY AS AGENT FOR THE AUTHOR, J.

REDMOND PRIOR WHO WAS UNKNOWN TO WARNER BROS. STUDIO PAID TWENTY

THOUSAND DOLLARS FOR THE STORY TITLED QUOTE THESE MANY YEARS UNQUOTE

AND ISSUED CHECK PAYABLE TO AUTHOR J. REDMOND PRIOR WHICH WAS TURNED

OVER TO GOLDSTONE AGENCY. CHECK WAS ENDORSED BY GOLDSTONE AGENCY AS

TRUSTEE FOR J. REDMOND PRIOR. STORY HAS SINCE BEEN MADE INTO

PICTURE QUOTE CHAINED LIGHTNING UNQUOTE STARRING HUMPHREY BOGART

COSTING ONE MILLION FOUR HUNDRED THOUSAND TO BE RELEASED IN ABOUT SIX

MONTHS. ██████ ABOUT TWO WEEKS AGO A ███████████ REPORTER BEGAN

CHECKING WITH STUDIO PUBLICITY DEPT. ALLEGING COLE THE AUTHOR AND

ASKING CONFIRMATION . SINCE THAT TIME THE STUDIO HAS BEEN CONDUCTING

OWN INVESTIGATION TO DETERMINE TRUTH OF ALLEGATION. THIS WAS STRAIGHT

STORY PURCHASE AND NO EMPLOYER DASH EMPLOYEE RELATIONSHIP INVOLVED

BETWEEN AUTHOR AND STUDIO. ████████████ PRESENTLY IN WASHINGTON D.C.

SUGGEST BUREAU DETERMINE WHETHER COLE-S FORTYEIGHT INCOME TAX RETURN

SHOWS ABOVE TWENTY THOUSAND DOLLAR PAYMENT, ALSO WHETHER INCOME TAX

MAY HAVE BEEN FILED UNDER NAME OF J. REDMOND PRIOR.

HOOD

END AND ACK

46-16420-5

NOV 17 1949

Lester Cole's FBI file reveals that the agency suspected that he may have failed to claim on his income tax return a payment of $20,000 for a movie he wrote under the pseudonym J. Redmond Prior.

under FBI surveillance abroad. Dmytryk, the FBI reported in one instance, "was in England where he was to work on a British film entitled 'Obsession' a comedy thriller based on a detective story."

Herbert Biberman, investigators noted, "has been active with other members of the Hollywood Ten in raising defense funds by various means. He has been observed by agents in contact with high ranking Communists in the Hollywood area, specifically at the home of ALBERT MALTZ." Samuel Ornitz was to lecture over four evenings to the Hollywood Women's Council about "The History of Anti-Semitism From Ancient to Modern Times— Looking Toward a Solution." Alvah Bessie "attended a meeting of the Steamfitters Local #250 [a union]." Ring Lardner Jr. was devoting his time to "writing activities" and "raising defense funds." Noting that Adrian Scott "appeared on the radio making a speech on October 18, 1948," the FBI reported that he was also busy raising funds and "attacking the Un-American Activities Committees, both state and national." John Howard Lawson, who was identified as the main contact for the Communist Party in the Los Angeles area, told a union meeting that his main reason for refusing to answer the HUAC's questions was that a "devotion to Americanism often calls for something other than conformity."

Individually or together, the Hollywood Ten filed eight lawsuits against their studios for breach of contract and conspiring to blacklist. Three of the cases were settled out of court; they lost the other five. Most of the judges were not sympathetic to their cause. The exception was Judge Leon Yankwich, who presided over Cole's suit against MGM. Yankwich denounced Eric Johnston as "dogmatic, doctrinaire, absolutist" and told MGM to reinstate Cole at his "$1,350-a-week job." Furthermore, he "ordered payment of $72,000 in [lost] salary." MGM appealed Yankwich's decision but later reached a settlement with Cole. Lardner's suit against Twentieth Century–Fox was settled out of court, as was the group's suit against the Motion Picture Association of America.

On June 13, 1949, in the U.S. Court of Appeals for the Federal Circuit, in Washington, DC, Judges Bennett Champ Clark, Wilbur K. Miller, and George C. Sweeney handed down their unanimous decision in Lawson and Trumbo's appeal of their convictions. Once again, attorneys for Lawson and Trumbo had taken "the position that Congress did not have a right to examine their political beliefs." The court ruled, "We hold that . . . Congress has power to make an inquiry of an individual which may elicit the answer that the witness is a believer in communism or a member of the Communist party." In other words, the HUAC was within its power to ask the men if they were or had ever been members of the Communist Party. As to the issue of the committee violating their First Amendment rights of free speech, free thought, and free association, the court explained, "It is fully established by . . . the Supreme Court that the right of free speech is not absolute, but must yield to national interests justifiably thought to be of larger importance. The same is true of the right to remain silent." The Hollywood Ten now put their fates in the hands of the nine justices of the Supreme Court of the United States.

But before they could proceed to the high court, dual tragedies struck. On July 19, Frank Murphy, a former governor of Michigan and one of the liberal Supreme Court justices, died of a heart attack. Less than two months later, Wiley B. Rutledge, another liberal on the court, died of a brain hemorrhage on September 10. "President Truman shockingly lowered the curtain on us," Lester Cole wrote, when he nominated two conservatives to fill the vacancies on the bench. With a conservative majority

John Howard Lawson leaving the federal court in Washington, DC, where he was convicted of contempt of Congress.

now on the Court, would the justices uphold the lower court's guilty verdicts, or would they support the men's First Amendment stand?

In an odd twist that amused the Hollywood Ten, on December 9, 1949, Representative J. Parnell Thomas, the man who had refused most of the unfriendly witnesses the opportunity to read their statements at the HUAC hearings, was in court on a fraud charge. He was accused of placing the "names of outsiders [nonworkers] on the payroll of his office. . . . These persons endorsed and delivered the Government pay checks, which they received from time to time, to [Thomas's] secretary." She, in turn, deposited the checks "to her own personal bank account" and wrote checks in equal amounts to Thomas. The representative pleaded no defense to the charge against him and was sentenced to six to eighteen months at the Federal Correctional Institution in Danbury, Connecticut. He was ordered to pay a fine of $10,000. In sentencing Thomas, Judge Alexander Holtzoff said that the former chairman of the House Committee on Un-American Activities should have been an example of "true Americanism" but failed.

On April 10, 1950, the Hollywood Ten glimpsed what lay ahead for them. The power of congressional committees to ask witnesses whether they were or were not members of the Communist Party "was upheld . . . when the Supreme Court refused to review the lower court convictions of John Howard Lawson and Dalton Trumbo." Their guilty verdicts would stand.

The Supreme Court's decision to uphold the lower court's convictions of Lawson and Trumbo was final and brought the Hollywood Ten to the end of their legal fight. Their lives would now be disrupted and their careers ruined as they awaited sentencing.

JOSEPH McCARTHY

On February 9, 1950, two months before the Supreme
Court handed down its decision on the Hollywood
Ten, Wisconsin senator Joseph McCarthy adopted the
methods of Red-baiting, or attacking a person or group
as being communistic, that was used by the House
Committee on Un-American Activities. While speaking
in Wheeling, West Virginia, the senator claimed to have
a list of 205 card-carrying communists employed by the
U.S. Department of State. After McCarthy's Wheeling
speech, the Senate called for a full investigation, which
cast the senator into the national spotlight—just as the
HUAC hearings had made J. Parnell Thomas a household
name. While the HUAC continued to look into Hollywood
and the Screen Writers Guild, McCarthy turned his
attention to the government, especially the State
Department. He leveled accusations against top officials
in the U.S. Army, including decorated war heroes. He also
went after labor union officials. Although a Soviet spy
ring was found at high levels of the government, most
of those accused by McCarthy were innocent victims.
Thousands of people lost their livelihoods and friends.
The end of the McCarthy era and McCarthyism came
on December 2, 1954, when the Senate condemned
McCarthy for dishonoring that legislative body.
The damage wrought by the House Committee on
Un-American Activities, however, continued unabated
for years after McCarthy's death in 1957.

Seven members of the Hollywood Ten arrive at the federal district court in Washington, DC, on June 22, 1950, to face charges stemming from their refusal to answer yes or no to the two primary questions asked by the House Committee on Un-American Activities. Seen here are, from

Lester Cole wrote that in the three years following his subpoena to appear in Washington in 1947, he and his wife "had sold three houses, each time buying a cheaper one." He also told a story about his eleven-year-old son, Michael, who listened in class as his teacher "spoke of how splendid our democratic system worked and that the Hollywood Ten would now surely go to jail." She apparently was the only one in class who was unaware that Michael's father was one of the ten. According to Cole, Michael raised his hand and said, "'You couldn't say that if you'd ever read the Constitution. Why don't you just read the First Amendment?' More than half the kids in the class applauded as Mike, tears in his eyes, walked out of the class and came home."

Like the others, director Edward Dmytryk "had hit a solid rock bottom. I knew exactly where I stood. I had no job, no money, no Directors Guild support." He had few remaining friends. He did the only thing he could think of: "I borrowed . . . from one of the few men I could still call friend."

Most of the Hollywood Ten experienced a similar situation, including quick sales of their homes and moves into cheaper and smaller housing. Many of their friends turned their backs on them, fearful that they, too, might be accused of being communists. Albert Maltz summed it up when he said, "We are financially and physically depleted."

By the end of September 1950, the futures of the ten film men had been settled. In June, Lawson and Trumbo were each fined $1,000. They left Washington's federal district court handcuffed to each other to begin serving one-year sentences at the federal penitentiary in Ashland, Kentucky. Six of the others received identical fines and sentences from the same judge. Facing a different judge, Biberman and Dmytryk were fined $1,000 each but sentenced to "only six months per culprit."

Of the ten, possibly only Dmytryk thought about changing the position he'd taken during the hearings and openly rejecting communism. He didn't do so at this time because he realized that changing course now and cooperating with the HUAC would appear false and self-serving. The others remained dedicated to their belief that they'd done the right thing, taken the true path. Upon entering the federal penitentiary in Texarkana, Texas, with Alvah Bessie, Biberman was asked by his parole adviser if he would still be uncooperative before the HUAC if given another chance. He said he would, because he believed the committee threatened the foundation of America's liberties.

Maltz and Dmytryk, "fitted with leg irons, handcuffs, and chained to each other," were taken to Mill Point, West Virginia. Samuel Ornitz served his time in Springfield, Missouri. Cole and Ring Lardner Jr. boarded a train to Danbury, Connecticut, where one of the first inmates they saw upon arriving at the prison was J. Parnell Thomas. Thomas had been assigned to work in the chicken coop. "His job," Cole wrote, "was to gather the eggs and scrape up the droppings." When Thomas saw Cole, he asked where his hammer and sickle were. Cole replied, "I see just like in Congress, you're still picking up chickenshit." The last of the ten to be sentenced, Adrian Scott, joined Lawson and Trumbo in Ashland.

After serving their sentences, the men had to scramble to provide for their families. Some of them returned to writing using pseudonyms. As Lardner wrote in a 1961 article for *Saturday Evening Post*, "A few of the writers among these outcasts have been able to operate under other names in the 'black market.' Others have had to find new occupations entirely,

After sentencing, John Howard Lawson (left) and Dalton Trumbo, both in front of the door, enter a U.S. Marshals Service van to be taken to prison.

among them carpentry, selling women's clothing, bartending, driving a school bus and waiting on tables in a restaurant." For the actors, directors, and producers, however, pseudonyms weren't an option; they couldn't put on masks and pretend to be somebody else. Some moved on to the theater in New York, but even there the HUAC was making its presence known.

While in prison, Dmytryk hoped to remove himself from the blacklist and from the Hollywood Ten. He wanted to return to directing movies. Just before his release, he wrote a statement in which he claimed, "I was not a communist or a communist sympathizer and . . . I had not been a communist at the time of the congressional hearings." It was witnessed by the prison warden on September 9, 1950, and did not mention any earlier involvement in the Communist Party. He saw this as the only way to move his career forward. He had a deal in the works with Columbia Pictures that would have paid him $60,000 per movie to start. Remembering this later, he wrote, "I dearly wished . . . that my prison statement had permanently removed me from the good graces of the communists in general and the Ten in particular."

Not long after his release, he opened his door one day to find Herbert Biberman standing outside. The other eight had not yet been released from prison, and Biberman wanted Dmytryk to write a letter of support to their parole boards urging early releases for the men. Reluctantly, as Dmytryk explained it, he agreed, on the condition that his "support could be made known only to the parole board; it was not to be released to the press." To his shock, two days later he found his name and support statement "splashed all over the front pages of both trade papers [the *Hollywood Reporter* and the *Daily Variety*]." Columbia Pictures withdrew its offer of work.

The House Committee on Un-American Activities, now under the chairmanship of Representative John S. Wood, resumed its focus on Hollywood in 1951. New hearings were held. After the convictions of the Hollywood Ten, no one argued that the First Amendment protected them from having to answer the committee's questions. Those who repented and said they were no longer communists were allowed to return to their jobs, as long as they informed on friends and coworkers. Those who did not were cited for contempt of Congress, unless they pleaded the Fifth Amendment, which most did. The Fifth Amendment provides that no person may be required to testify against himself or herself. Although taking the Fifth implies no guilt in a legal sense, in the minds of many Americans it does. Those who pleaded the Fifth became known as Fifth Amendment communists. Hollywood's bosses decided that these witnesses should also be blacklisted. "This blacklisted status, expanded to cover more than 400 people from various crafts in movies, television and radio, . . . persisted," Lardner wrote in 1961.

When actor Larry Parks, one of the original nineteen unfriendly witnesses, took the stand in March 1951, he begged the HUAC (now also known as the Wood Committee) not to make him identify other members of the Communist Party. He was willing to talk about his own brief involvement, but he didn't wish to hurt other people who in his opinion had done nothing wrong. "To force a man to do this is not American justice," he said. Ultimately, he named members of the Communist Party in a closed-door hearing. Even so, he was blacklisted and could no longer find work in Hollywood. The studio he worked for refused to release a movie he had completed, shelving it for several years.

When Dmytryk made his second appearance before the

Movie director Edward Dmytryk before the House Committee on Un-American Activities a second time, in April 1951. In this appearance, he said that he'd left the Communist Party before the 1947 hearings and gave the committee the names of twenty-six other Hollywood communists.

HUAC on April 25, 1951, and identified twenty-six others as communists—people the committee already knew about—he appeared contrite and ashamed. Although he maintained that he'd left the Communist Party before the 1947 hearings and accused the eighteen other unfriendly witnesses of bullying him to go along with their plan to be uncooperative with the committee, several others remembered it differently. They recalled that Dmytryk was active in the party throughout the hearings and that he was a willing participant in the group's unbending desire to put the HUAC out of business. Robert W. Kenny, one of the attorneys for the nineteen men, also disagreed with Dmytryk's claim that they had refused to answer the committee's questions. In a letter to Albert Maltz in 1973, Kenny, then a Los Angeles Superior Court judge, wrote, "The Ten stoutly maintained that they were *not refusing* to testify. They merely wanted to answer the committee in their own way. This created a jury issue as to whether they had actually refused or had been prematurely removed from the witness stand by the short-fused Chairman, Parnell Thomas." Whatever the case may be, Dmytryk was able to resume his career, though at the cost of numerous friendships.

Still, the hearings continued. Screenwriter and playwright Lillian Hellman took the stand on May 21, 1952. She had been blacklisted since 1947, but she responded to the summons to appear before the committee with an open letter to Chairman Wood on May 19. She wrote, "I am most willing to answer all questions about myself. I have nothing to hide from your Committee and there is nothing in my life of which I am ashamed." She went on to say she was willing to waive her right to plead the Fifth Amendment "if your Committee will agree to refrain from asking me to name other people." The committee rejected her offer. When asked to name names, Hellman refused, citing the Fifth Amendment. While she continued to write for the stage, she was blacklisted in Hollywood.

Numerous vigilante groups sprang up after the 1947 hearings. They made it their business to target communists and sympathizers, both inside and outside the film industry, with or without evidence. The names they provided became the basis for what was known as the graylist, as opposed to those who found themselves blacklisted for not cooperating with the HUAC. The book *Red Channels* was first published by three ex-FBI agents in 1947. It listed 151 names of Hollywood entertainers whom the agents considered un-American. New names were added on a regular basis. Studio heads paid attention, and people whose names appeared in the publication saw their work quietly dry up. The Wage Earners Committee published the *National Wage Earner*, which listed movies the group considered communist-leaning. Aware, Inc., formed by onetime New York actors, published *Confidential Notebook*, which also contained the names of actors believed to be Reds. *The American Legion* magazine put out a publication, similar to *Red Channels*, that named people it thought were too liberal to be truly American.

All of these groups identified individuals, organizations, and industries they thought should be boycotted. Mistakes were made, however, and people were incorrectly identified. In 1954, *The American Legion* confused screenwriter Louis Pollock "with Louis Pollack, a California clothier, who had refused to cooperate with HUAC." Pollock saw his career suddenly evaporate because of this mistake. He eventually cleared his name in 1959, but his career never recovered.

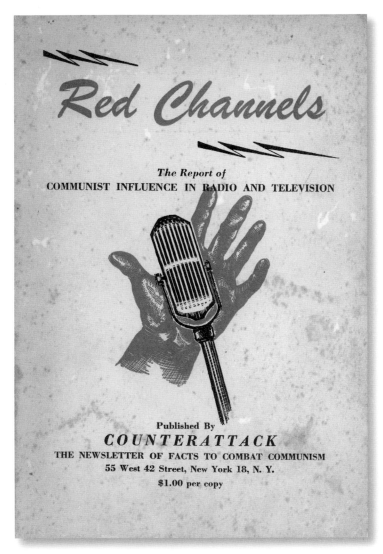

The book *Red Channels* targeted people, organizations, and written works that its publishers believed were communists or sympathetic to communism. The 1950 edition shown here listed the names of hundreds of suspected communists in its 214 pages, including actor Lee J. Cobb, for his participation in an auction that benefited the *Daily Worker*, a Communist Party newspaper; actor José Ferrer, for belonging to the American Committee for Protection of Foreign Born and for contributing to the National Committee to Abolish the HUAC; and writer Dashiell Hammett, for signing a petition to the Supreme Court to review the convictions of John Howard Lawson and Dalton Trumbo.

While Pollock was trying to figure out why he was suddenly unemployable, actor and comedian Samuel Joel "Zero" Mostel was subpoenaed to appear before the committee in August 1955. Mostel's nightclub act made fun of Red-baiters. He also played supporting roles in movies produced by Twentieth Century–Fox, but he suddenly found his contract canceled when the studio learned he was about to be named as a communist. He was then blacklisted in Hollywood, though he continued to find work in New York on the stage. When he testified before the committee, Mostel was playful but still bitter at being blacklisted. He referred to his former employer as "Eighteenth Century-Fox." When asked if he'd ever been a member of the Young Communist League, the youth wing of the Communist Party USA, Mostel pleaded the Fifth Amendment and later refused to discuss anyone but himself. The Hollywood studios continued to blacklist him until 1959, when he was finally cast in a television program.

Mostel, Pollock, Hellman, and Parks were just a few of the people swept up by the Committee on Un-American Activities in the years after the Hollywood Ten were convicted and the studios issued the Waldorf Statement. Denied employment, they were blacklisted. The list grew into the hundreds and included not only actors, writers, directors, and producers, but also set designers, lighting technicians, and others in the trades. It included the spouses of those who were blacklisted when they refused to testify against their husbands or wives. Yet these individuals had committed no crimes. They had broken no laws. They hadn't advocated the overthrow of the U.S. government. They were simply caught up in the hysteria surrounding the Cold War.

In 1954, *Roman Holiday* won an Academy Award for best motion picture story. Ian McLellan Hunter, an English

Actor and comedian Zero Mostel found work on the New York stage in productions such as *Fiddler on the Roof*, but he was blacklisted in Hollywood until 1959.

screenwriter, was credited with writing the story and accepted the Oscar. But Dalton Trumbo actually wrote it while living in Mexico following his release from prison. Unable to find work in Hollywood, Trumbo had arranged to have Hunter front for him. It was a way for him to keep some money coming in while also keeping the studio bosses in the dark about who was really behind this and other stories.

Trumbo had another win for best motion picture story in 1957. The movie, *The Brave One*, was written under one of Trumbo's pseudonyms, Robert Rich. When Rich's name was announced at the awards ceremony and he wasn't there to accept his Oscar, rumors began to circulate around Hollywood as to his true identity. It was then that Trumbo saw a way of attacking the blacklist. He began a campaign of whispers, hints, and rumors that he might be the difficult-to-find writer, but when asked directly, he said later he would "refuse either to confirm or to deny" the speculation. In this way, he was able to undermine the entire movie industry. "In fact," Ring Lardner Jr. wrote, "he maintained an astute policy of refusing to deny the authorship of any picture, and his name was attached by gossip to more screenplays than even as energetic a man as he could turn out." Industry policy prohibited blacklisted writers from being eligible to win an Academy Award, but then the screenplay for *The Defiant Ones* was nominated for one in 1959. It had been cowritten by two authors—one blacklisted, one not. To be fair to the author who was not blacklisted, the Academy of Motion Picture Arts and Sciences was forced to reverse its policy and nominate both writers. A few days after these nominations were announced in January, Trumbo came forward as the hard-to-locate Robert Rich. With this, the blacklist began to unravel.

Director Otto Preminger hired Trumbo in 1959 to write the screenplay for the movie *Exodus*. A rarity in Hollywood, Preminger had complete control over his films. He answered to no one. In an era when blacklisted writers' names were removed from the films they'd previously written and now were writing under false idenentities, Preminger announced on January 20, 1960, in a *New York Times* article that Trumbo's name would appear on the screen. Whether it was Preminger's action that inspired him or something he had already decided to do, actor and producer Kirk Douglas then gave credit to Trumbo for the film *Spartacus*, in which, according to Ring Lardner Jr.'s son James, "Trumbo tied the civil rights and civil liberties struggles of his own time . . . to a fight that went back two thousand years."

Although Trumbo's on-screen credits marked the official end of the Hollywood blacklist, it continued unofficially into the 1970s.

AFTER THEIR FALL

While the original blacklist included only the ten witnesses who defied the HUAC by attempting to answer its questions in their own ways, it eventually grew to include hundreds in the entertainment industry and many more in the world beyond the movie capital. Some of the Hollywood Ten eventually returned to work under their own names; most did not. None ever regained his former success.

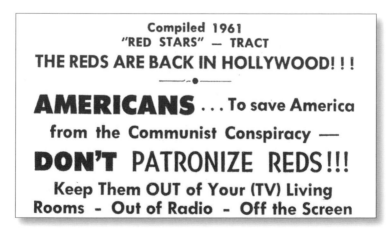

Pamphlets of "Red Stars" distributed to the public encouraged readers to combat communism on TV, on radio, and in the movies by boycotting broadcasts and films.

Samuel Ornitz was a vocal supporter of the USSR and politically outspoken. He, along with Lester Cole and John Howard Lawson, had been founding members of the Screen Writers Guild. His novel *Bride of the Sabbath* was published while he was in prison for his contempt of Congress conviction, but he never again wrote for motion pictures. He continued to write novels and died of cancer in 1957.

Both Herbert Biberman and his wife, the Oscar-winning actress Gale Sondergaard, were blacklisted after Biberman served his time. Sondergaard was blacklisted because she supported her husband during the hearings. Biberman never worked in Hollywood again, but in 1953 he teamed up with other blacklisted artists to direct *Salt of the Earth*, a picture based on the 1951 miners' strike against the Empire Zinc Company in New Mexico. The House of Representatives called the movie subversive and sympathetic to communism because it supported the workers. The *Hollywood Reporter* said, without evidence, that it had been made on direct orders from Russian leaders. The powerful and conservative American Legion called for a nationwide boycott of the film. Hollywood did everything within its power to prevent the motion picture from being made and shown. Even so, a limited number of theaters allowed it to run. Biberman released the film in Europe, where it received honors and awards. In 1992, the Library of Congress added it to the National Film Registry, which was established to ensure the survival and conservation of films deemed important to America's heritage. Biberman died of bone cancer in 1971. Sondergaard remained blacklisted until 1968, when she was cast in *Savage Intruder*, which was released in 1970. She last appeared on film in 1983 and died in 1985.

Producer Adrian Scott sued RKO Radio Pictures for wrongful

suspension, and the case made it all the way to the U.S. Supreme Court, where conservative justices rejected it in 1957. After serving his prison sentence, he found work in England writing for television, but without credit. After Trumbo received on-screen acknowledgment for *Exodus* and *Spartacus*, Scott returned to Los Angeles, where he was hired by Universal Studios. Using his wife's name, Joanne Court, he wrote for television, including for shows such as *Lassie* and *Have Gun—Will Travel*. He died of lung cancer in 1972.

After being blacklisted, Dalton Trumbo moved his family to Mexico for a time, where he wrote under various pseudonyms. He was a good writer and could write quickly in various genres. After his return from Mexico in 1953, he became "a kind of central clearinghouse for black market work." He never turned down a job, and if he couldn't do the work himself, he sent it on to other blacklisted writers so they could keep a roof over their head. His son, Chris, commented later that his father "used at least 13 different names and had an elaborate bank account system to protect himself and the producers from being detected. When I was 16 or 17, I was running around town with sometimes $10,000 or $20,000 in cash and checks, depositing them under these different names." In 1970, the guild that had once shunned him awarded him its Laurel Award for Screenwriting Achievement. *Papillon* (1973) was his last screenwriting credit. A six-pack-a-day smoker, Trumbo was diagnosed with lung cancer in 1973 and died of heart failure in 1976.

John Howard Lawson, the first president of the Screen Writers Guild, was "the head of the Hollywood cell of the Communist Party." His son Jeffrey said that his father "was an idealist. He really believed Marxism [communism] would make a better society." After being released from prison, Lawson went to Mexico, where he wrote books on filmmaking. Using a pseudonym, he co-wrote the screenplays for an anti-apartheid movie based on the book *Cry, the Beloved Country*, released in 1951, and *The Careless Years* (1957), his last screenplay. He died in 1977 of complications from Parkinson's disease, a disorder that left him with tremors and impaired balance.

After his time in prison, Albert Maltz moved to Mexico to write. Seventeen American publishers rejected his novel *A Long Day in a Short Life*, which he wrote while living there. Even Little, Brown and Company, which had published three of his earlier books, refused him. Foreign publishers, however, were open to his work, and the book sold well in England, where the HUAC hearings and the sentences of the Hollywood Ten were thought to be an example of American insanity. In 1960, singer and actor Frank Sinatra defied the blacklist and hired Maltz to write a screen adaptation of *The Execution of Private Slovik*. But when Sinatra was attacked by the Hearst newspapers, the American Legion, and other conservative groups, he was forced to fire Maltz. The screenwriter wrote several motion picture scripts for which he received no credit, but in 1970 producers finally agreed to acknowledge him for his work on *Two Mules for Sister Sara*, a Western starring Clint Eastwood. Maltz died in 1985.

Alvah Bessie said that he "was thrown out of Hollywood" after the HUAC hearings and "[had] been involved in a struggle to stay alive ever since." Upon his release from prison, he refused to write under an assumed name. He worked instead as a publicist for arts organizations, a book reviewer, an editor for a union newspaper, and a lighting technician for the hungry i, a nightclub in San Francisco. He died in 1985.

Lester Cole (center) with his son Michael and wife, Jonnie (Jeanne),
at a rally to support the Hollywood Ten.

Lester Cole said that he "went from a handsome contract at M-G-M in 1947 to working as a waiter in New York in 1951." In 1961, he moved to England, where, under the name Gerald L. C. Copley, he wrote the screen adaptation of Joy Adamson's book *Born Free*, which was released in 1966. But the blacklist destroyed Cole financially and broke up his family. While he was working on one black-market project, an executive producer dropped a hint as to how he might get off the list: "To use my own name, all I had to do was write a letter swearing I was no longer a Commie. . . . I said, no, I'd use a pseudonym." He continued to remain true to his beliefs, later relocating to San Francisco, where he taught film writing at the University of California. In a letter to the editor of the *New York Times* in 1978, he commented on the Hollywood Ten's use of the First Amendment as a defense for not answering the HUAC's questions in the way the committee wanted: "In April 1977, the Supreme Court (Wooley vs. Maynard) ruled we were right. Chief Justice [Warren E.] Burger wrote: 'The right to speak freely and the right to refrain from speaking at all are both protected by the First Amendment.' A belated but gratifying vindication." Although he later thought about trying to have his conviction overturned, the statute of limitations had run out; it was too late for justice. He died of a heart attack in 1985.

After Edward Dmytryk washed his hands of communism and appeared before the HUAC a second time to name names, he rebounded from his time on the Hollywood blacklist. Yet his decision to inform on others overshadowed the rest of his life; many in the Hollywood community, especially among the Hollywood Ten, refused to forgive him. Still, he had movies to direct. *The Caine Mutiny* and *Raintree County* came out in the mid-1950s, followed by *The Carpetbaggers* in the mid-1960s.

After his directing career tapered off in the 1970s, he taught film theory and production at the University of Texas at Austin. In 1981, he began teaching filmmaking at the University of Southern California in Los Angeles. He died of kidney and heart failure in 1999.

Ring Lardner Jr. was able to place his book, *The Ecstasy of Owen Muir*, with a little-known American publisher, but it was ignored by reviewers and boycotted by most bookstores. It proved to be popular in England, however. When he shared his biographical information with his British publisher and admitted to being one of the Hollywood Ten, he was pleasantly surprised at the reaction: "There may possibly be some publicity value, at least in this country, on account of this fact." Subsequently, Lardner, like so many other blacklisted writers, began writing under assumed names. "The people for whom I was directly working knew who I was," he wrote later, "but the men who signed the checks in some instances did not." It wasn't until the mid-1960s that he was hired to co-write the screenplay for *The Cincinnati Kid* using his own name. In 1971, he won an Oscar, his second, for his screen adaptation of Richard Hooker's comic novel *MASH*, on which the long-running television series also was based. He wrote only two more screenplays during his lifetime. The last of the Hollywood Ten to die, he passed away on October 31, 2000.

The long-lived House of Representatives' Committee on Un-American Activities instilled fear in both Hollywood and the American public. Hundreds, if not thousands, from the motion picture industry, government, and business were swept into a new category—the nonentity, the nonperson. Neighbors leveled accusations against neighbors. Workers informed on fellow workers. The lesson was to speak carefully, never criticize the United States or any representative of the government, and conform. Mostly conform—don't be different.

In 1969, the House Committee on Un-American Activities was renamed the House Committee on Internal Security, which continued investigating the lives of both celebrities and ordinary citizens until January 14, 1975, when it was abolished. Actor Robert Vaughn questioned how the HUAC could happen in the United States in his 1972 book *Only Victims*: "The First Amendment prohibits Congress from passing any laws abridging the freedoms of religion, speech, press, assembly and petition. Yet HUAC's total thrust was to investigate the written or spoken flow of ideas that it considered 'un-American,' a term that defies definition."

Almost from its very beginning in 1938 under Chairman Martin Dies Jr., the House Committee on Un-American Activities faced opposition for looking into people's private lives and for the heavy-handed ways in which it did so. As a committee of Congress, it wasn't obligated to follow the rules that any U.S. court of law had to observe.

While most of the Hollywood Ten rejected communism in the years that followed their imprisonment, none ever wanted to see the United States adopt an authoritarian government or become like Russia. They valued the Constitution and its Bill of Rights. They appreciated America's free enterprise system and the power of the vote. What they saw in the Communist Party was

Published a week after the Hollywood Ten finished their testimony, political cartoons criticized the way the men had been treated, including being abruptly dismissed from the witness stand and not being allowed to read their statements fully or at all.

the promise of more equality between employers and workers and a recognition of workers' unions. They sought racial fairness and religious freedom at a time when the country was ignoring its constitutional guarantee of equality. One hundred fifty-nine films were credited to the Hollywood Ten between 1929 and 1949; none of these contained communist propaganda. Today, the Blacklist Credit Committee of the Writers Guild of America, West, is working to properly credit the films of the Hollywood Ten and other blacklisted writers. What happened to the Hollywood Ten, to the hundreds of others who were blacklisted, and to the nation as a whole was a failure of democracy—a failure of both elected leaders and those who elected them to uphold the freedoms that Americans have championed from the earliest days of these United States.

AUTHOR'S NOTE

The Vietnam War and the U.S. fight against the spread of communism in that Southeast Asian country was winding down when I began my teaching career in 1971, but the Cold War and the remnants of the decades-long hearings of the House Committee on Un-American Activities still lingered. One of the documents I signed, in addition to my teaching contract (for a whopping $8,700 a year), was a loyalty oath—a pledge to fight all enemies foreign and domestic. I signed it without giving any thought to what it said or the history behind it. It wasn't until I began researching this book that I began to understand that loyalty oath, along with the political positions of the Hollywood Ten and why they made the brave stand they did.

As I delved into the lives and times of these blacklisted men, I was struck by the strong similarities between then and now. The U.S. was in a cold war with a political enemy—the USSR—whose economic ideas differed from our own, and fear was everywhere. Because Americans were told that national interests dictated their necessity, the HUAC hearings moved forward without much constraint from lawmakers and others. The FBI regularly looked into the lives of ordinary citizens if even a hint of suspicion was raised. The gulf between the haves and the have-nots was wide. Some politicians called for strengthened immigration laws. Many suggested that those who didn't conform to the political norms of the U.S. should be deported, just as tens of thousands of Mexican immigrants and Mexican Americans had been deported during the Great Depression of the 1930s. Segregation was a fixture in most of the country, and it applied not only to African Americans but also to anyone else who wasn't white and Protestant.

Is it so different today? The United States is still at odds with Russia, and a new enemy—terrorism—has emerged, with national interest cited as an excuse to investigate individuals and groups of people. It may well be that in order to protect America in the twenty-first century, it is necessary to collect information on its citizens, but should the government be required to prove probable cause before conducting probes, and should other restrictions apply? Should these inquiries be made with the purpose of publicly embarrassing individuals and damaging reputations, as they were during the HUAC hearings, or should some discretion be used? Newt Gingrich, a former politician, has even suggested that the country needs a new House Committee on Un-American Activities. Would that be wise? We live in a country where the gap between the wealthy and the rest of society is wider than it has been in recent memory, where new immigrants are blamed for the country's woes (just as they have been throughout our history), and where there is talk of building a wall along the country's southern border. Seldom, though, is anything said about the country's porous northern border. Is this an issue of security or bigotry? There are calls to deport some and deny refuge to others. Racial, ethnic, and religious biases are being voiced more loudly than in the recent past—a troubling issue for many who thought prejudice was a part only of the country's darker history. These are some of the questions and issues we need to explore as Americans.

Ring Lardner Jr. was once asked if he thought blacklists would ever be used in this country again, and he said he didn't think it would be possible. I'm not as certain as Mr. Lardner, but I am hopeful. America and Americans need to be ever watchful that the Constitution's guarantees are never sacrificed again out of fear, hysteria, prejudice, or political passion.

BIBLIOGRAPHY

SOURCES CONSULTED BY THE AUTHOR

Bessie, Alvah. *Inquisition in Eden*. New York: Macmillan, 1965.

Ceplair, Larry, and Steven Englund. *The Inquisition in Hollywood: Politics in the Film Community, 1930–60*. Urbana: University of Illinois Press, 2003. First published 1970 by University of Illinois Press.

Cole, Lester. *Hollywood Red: The Autobiography of Lester Cole*. Palo Alto, CA: Ramparts Press, 1981.

Dmytryk, Edward. *Odd Man Out: A Memoir of the Hollywood Ten*. Carbondale: Southern Illinois University Press, 1996.

Hearings Regarding the Communist Infiltration of the Motion Picture Industry: Hearings Before the Committee on Un-American Activities, House of Representatives, 80th Cong., 1st sess., October 20, 21, 22, 23, 24, 27, 28, 29, and 30, 1947. Washington, DC: U.S. Government Printing Office, 1947 (HUAC 1947).

Horne, Gerald. *The Final Victim of the Blacklist: John Howard Lawson, Dean of the Hollywood Ten*. Berkeley: University of California Press, 2006.

Investigation of Communist Activities, New York Area—Part VIII (Entertainment): Hearing before the Committee on Un-American Activities, House of Representatives, 84th Cong., 1st sess., October 14, 1955. Washington, DC: U.S. Government Printing Office, 1955.

Kahn, Gordon. *Hollywood on Trial: The Story of the 10 Who Were Indicted*. New York: Boni & Gaer, 1948.

Lardner, Ring, Jr. *I'd Hate Myself in the Morning: A Memoir*. New York: Thunder's Mouth Press/Nation Books, 2000.

Navasky, Victor S. *Naming Names*. New York: Hill and Wang, 2003.

Trumbo, Dalton. *The Time of the Toad: A Study of Inquisition in America*. Repr. ed. London: Journeyman Press, 1982. First published by the Hollywood Ten, 1949.

Vaughn, Robert. *Only Victims: A Study of Show Business Blacklisting*. New York: Limelight Editions, 1996.

Useful material also was found in assorted newspapers and magazines, including the following: *Brooklyn Daily Eagle, Hollywood Reporter, Los Angeles Times, Los Angeles Times Magazine, New Republic, Newsweek, New York Daily News, New York Times, Saturday Evening Post,* and *Washington Post.* Additional details and quotations were gleaned from the Lester Cole Papers and Lester Cole's FBI file (both courtesy of Michael and Sheila Cole) and from letters, articles, and other documents held in the archives of the Margaret Herrick Library, Academy of Motion Picture Arts and Sciences, Beverly Hills, CA, as well as from the National Archives and Records Administration, Washington, DC.

FILMS/VIDEOS

Committee on UnAmerican Activities. A film by Robert Carl Cohen, 1962, 2005. DVD, Radical Films, 2002.

Hollywood on Trial. Directed by David Helpern Jr. Corinth Films, 1976.

McCarthy Years. Edward R. Murrow Collection. Hosted by Walter Cronkite. CBS, 1991. DVD, New Video Group, 2005.

Salt of the Earth. A film by Michael Wilson, Herbert Biberman, and Paul Jarrico. Independent Production Corporation and International Union of Mine, Mill and Smelter Workers, 1954. DVD, Pioneer Entertainment, 1999.

Trumbo. Directed by Jay Roach. Bleecker Street Films, ShivHans Pictures, and Groundswell Productions, 2015.

Trumbo. Directed by Peter Askin. Trumbo Films, 2007. DVD, Magnolia Home Entertainment, 2009.

WEBSITES*

Blackerby, Christine. "Pleading the Fifth: Lillian Hellman and the HUAC Investigation of Hollywood." *Social Education* 80, no 6 (2016): 316–20. https://www.socialstudies.org/publications/socialeducation/november-december2016/pleading-fifth-lillian-hellman-and-huac-investigation-of-hollywood.

Dunbar, David L. "The Hollywood Ten: The Men Who Refused to Name Names." *Hollywood Reporter*. http://www.hollywoodreporter.com/lists/hollywood-ten-men-who-refused-839762.

"Guide to House Records: Chapter 22: 1910–1946 Nazi and Other Propaganda." Sect. 22.87. National Archives. http://www.archives.gov/legislative/guide/house/chapter-22-select-propaganda.html.

Hoffer, Chrystal. "The Birth of Anticommunist National Rhetoric: The Fish Committee Hearings in 1930s Seattle." The Great Depression in Washington State: Pacific Northwest Labor and Civil Rights Projects, University of Washington. http://depts.washington.edu/depress/fish_committee.shtml.

"Hollywood Blacklist." United States History. http://www.u-s-history.com/pages/h1850.html.

"Hollywood Blacklist." *Wikipedia*. https://en.wikipedia.org/wiki/Hollywood_blacklist.

*Websites active at time of publication

"The Hollywood Ten." History.com. http://www.history.com/topics/cold-war/hollywood-ten.

"Hollywood Ten." Spartacus Educational. http://spartacus-educational.com/USAhollywood10.htm.

"The House Un-American Activities Committee." *Hollywood Reporter*. http://www.hollywoodreporter.com/lists/hollywood-ten-men-who-refused-839762.

"The House Un-American Activities Committee (HUAC)" and "The Cold War: Investigating the Red Menace." History.com. http://www.history.com/topics/cold-war/huac.

"House Un-American Activities Committee." *Wikipedia*. https://en.wikipedia.org/wiki/House_Un-American_Activities_Committee.

"Kilbourn v. Thompson." *Oxford Reference*. http://www.oxfordreference.com/view/10.1093/oi/authority.20110803100036451.

ACKNOWLEDGMENTS

I'm inclined to believe that whoever said writing is a solitary profession never wrote. Certainly, the act of putting words on paper or computer screen is solitary and, for me, requires absolute silence, but accumulating the resources that inform those words and the act of polishing a manuscript is anything but isolated. I am indebted to so many people for helping me along my journey from blank screen, to multiple rough drafts over the past two years, to what you are now reading. First, my thanks go out to Louise Hilton, research specialist, Special Collections, Margaret Herrick Library, Academy of Motion Picture Arts and Sciences; Marisa Duron, Special Collections, Margaret Herrick Library, Academy of Motion Picture Arts and Sciences; Rachel Bernstein, reference librarian, Margaret Herrick Library, Academy of Motion Picture Arts and Sciences; and the entire staff at this valuable archive for answering my endless questions, collecting materials, pointing me in the right direction, chasing down inaccurately labeled resource references, and running copies—which freed me to stick my nose into yet more files. I also thank Lisa Schloss, librarian, Social Science, Philosophy and Religion Department, Los Angeles Public Library; the History and Genealogy Department staff,

Los Angeles Public Library; and Steve Nycklemoe, director of operations, The Hollywood Museum. A bushel of gratitude goes to Barbara Hall, independent film historian and researcher, for vetting the manuscript, despite its being in very rough form. (I was embarrassed when I realized it was not the draft I intended to send her.) Barbara's thoughtful and gentle comments aided in shaping the final manuscript. Thanks to David M. Hardy, section chief, Record/Information Dissemination Section, Records Management Division, Federal Bureau of Investigation; and Adam Berenbak, archivist, Center for Legislative Archives, National Archives and Records Administration, who offered information about files and records pertaining to the Hollywood Ten. Thanks also to Ann Trevor, independent researcher, National Archives and Records Administration, who tracked down information vital to the story when I was unable to travel. A shout-out to Susan Robertson, librarian, Dolores County (Colorado) Public Library, Rico Branch, for library access before, during, and after hours; this book wouldn't have been completed without her generosity. As always, I am grateful to Carolyn P. Yoder and the editorial and design crew at Calkins Creek Books. Thanks also to the Lardner clan, Niki Trumbo, and Dan Bessie for responding so promptly and graciously to my pleas for help. Finally, my heartfelt thanks to Michael and Sheila Cole for opening their garage and the boxes containing Lester Cole's screenplays, contracts, FBI files, clippings, correspondence, and so much more. I hope this story of the Hollywood Ten meets with their approval.

SOURCE NOTES

The source of each quotation in this book is found below. The citation indicates the first words of the quotation and its document source. The sources are listed either in the bibliography or below.

FRONT MATTER
"If a man . . .": Trumbo, *The Time of the Toad*, p. 25.
"It is a very . . .": Kahn, p. 203.

CHAPTER 1
"investigation into . . .": J. Parnell Thomas, *Hearings Regarding the Communist Infiltration of the Motion Picture Industry* (hereafter cited as HUAC 1947), p. 1.
"like that on . . .": Kahn, p. 5.
"The act of subverting . . .": "Subversion," Merriam-Webster.com, n.d., http://www.merriam-webster.com/dictionary/subversion, accessed June 24, 2016.
"five cameras": "Red Probe on Today; 50 Called," *Hollywood Reporter*, October 20, 1947, p. 1. (Sourced because the number varies from five to eight to dozens.)
"Four majors . . .": Ibid.
"Press arrangements . . .": Ibid.
"twelve screenwriters . . .": Kahn, p. 5.

"The fear, chaos . . .": Cole, p. 266.

"several surprises": J. Parnell Thomas, quoted in "Red Probe," p. 11.

"The committee . . .": Thomas, HUAC 1947, p. 1.

"With such vast . . .": Ibid.

"volunteers of information": J. Parnell Thomas, quoted in Ceplair and Englund, p. 255.

"Americanism . . .": Ibid.

"There is no question . . .": Thomas, HUAC 1947, p. 2.

"Mr. Chairman, I . . .": Robert W. Kenny, HUAC 1947, p. 3.

"May we ask . . .": Bartley C. Crum, HUAC 1947, p. 4.

"You may not . . .": Thomas, HUAC 1947, p. 4.

"You are not . . .": Quoted by Lela Rogers, HUAC 1947, p. 4.

"unfriendly": "Red Probe," p. 11.

"Congress may conduct . . ." and "the private affairs . . .": "Kilbourn v. Thompson," *Oxford Reference*, http://www.oxfordreference.com/view/10.1093/oi/authority.20110803100036451, accessed September 14, 2016.

"Mr. Chairman, if you . . .": Kenny, HUAC 1947, p. 287.

"Mr. Chairman, may I . . .": Crum, HUAC 1947, p. 289.

"Mr. Kenny . . .": Thomas, HUAC 1947, p. 289.

"The request . . .": Thomas, HUAC 1947, p. 289.

"A copy . . .": Kahn, p. 68.

"I don't care . . .": Thomas, HUAC 1947, p. 290.

"You refuse . . .": John Howard Lawson, HUAC 1947, p. 290.

"I refuse . . .": Thomas, HUAC 1947, p. 290.

"For a week . . .": John Howard Lawson, quoted in Vaughn, p. 327.

"Are you . . .": Robert E. Stripling, HUAC 1947, p. 291.

"mostly in the . . .": Jack Warner, HUAC 1947, p. 12.

"The raising . . .": Lawson, HUAC 1947, p. 291.

"Mr. Chairman—": Stripling, HUAC 1947, p. 291.

"Is absolutely . . .": Lawson, HUAC 1947, p. 291.

"Mr. Chairman—": Stripling, HUAC 1947, p. 291.

"But—": Lawson, HUAC 1947, p. 291.

"It is a matter . . .": Ibid.

"I am not . . .: Ibid.

"I am glad . . .": Lawson, HUAC 1947, p. 292.

"Mr. Lawson, are you . . .": Stripling, HUAC 1947, p. 293.

CHAPTER 2

"inspired fear . . .": Crystal Hoffer, "The Birth of Anticommunist
    National Rhetoric: The Fish Committee Hearings in 1930s
    Seattle," The Great Depression in Washington State: Pacific
    Northwest Labor and Civil Rights Projects, University of
    Washington, http://depts.washington.edu/depress/fish_committee.
    shtml, accessed August 18, 2016.

"worked to establish . . .": "Guide to House Records: Chapter 22:
    1910–1946 Nazi and Other Propaganda," sect. 22.87, National
    Archives, http://www.archives.gov/legislative/guide/house/chapter-
    22-select-propaganda.html, accessed August 17, 2016.

"a branch . . ." and "infested with . . .": J. Parnell Thomas, quoted in
    "Theatre Project Faces an Inquiry," New York Times, July 27,
    1938.

"Practically every play . . .": Ibid.

"American tradition of . . .": Ellen Woodward, quoted in "WPA Plays
    Upheld at Dies Hearing," New York Times, December 6, 1938.

"adopted the practice . . ." and "a threat to . . .": Donald Ogden
    Stewart, quoted in "Anti-Nazi Leaguers Fight Red Aid Charge,"
    Los Angeles Times, August 16, 1938.

"It is an ominous . . .": Dorothy Parker, quoted ibid.

"We are busy . . .": John W. Considine Jr., quoted in "Hollywood
    League Demands That 'Red' Charge Be Proved," Los Angeles
    Times, August 18, 1938.

"may defeat . . .": Franklin D. Roosevelt, quoted in "Roosevelt Warns
    Dies His Methods Endanger Justice," New York Times, November
    28, 1940.

CHAPTER 3

"Mr. Lawson, are you . . .": Stripling, HUAC 1947, p. 293.

"in the early . . .": Dmytryk, p. 59n.

"His personality . . .": Horne, p. 3.

"In a nation . . .": Ibid.

"man who seldom . . .": Jeffrey Lawson, quoted ibid.

"In framing . . .": Lawson, HUAC 1947, p. 293.

"It soon . . .": Cole, p. 280.

"The question . . .": Lawson, HUAC 1947, p. 294.

"in order to create . . .": Ibid.

"If you want . . .": Ibid.

"We are going . . .": Thomas, HUAC 1947, p. 294.

"It is unfortunate . . .": Lawson, HUAC 1947, p. 294.

"[Lawson] was . . .": Kahn, p. 47.

"That is not . . .": Thomas, HUAC 1947, p. 294.

"Excuse . . .": Ibid., p. 295.

"Stand away . . .": Ibid.

"I have written . . .": Lawson, HUAC 1947, p. 295.

"take this man . . .": Thomas, HUAC 1947, p. 295.

"official organ": Stripling, HUAC 1947, p. 295.

"What did your . . .": Ibid., p. 296.

"During the course . . .": Louis J. Russell, HUAC 1947, p. 296.

"Neither I . . ." and "We deplored . . .": Lardner, pp. 6–7.

"It was unnecessary . . .": Dmytryk, p. 60.

"never be . . .": Eric Johnston, quoted in Kahn, p. 6.

"A damaging impression . . .": Eric Johnston, HUAC 1947, p. 306.

"Our freedoms . . .": Ibid., p. 307.

"It . . . is getting . . .": Ibid., p. 308.

"crypto-fascists": "Pepper Asks Fight to Save Liberties," *New York Times*, October 27, 1947.

"twenty-five prominent . . .": Gladwin Hill, "Stars Fly to Fight Inquiry into Films," *New York Times*, October 27, 1947.

"the inquiry of . . .": Ibid.

"denouncing the inquiry . . .": Ibid.

"four democratic senators . . .": Ibid.

"We question . . .": Myrna Loy, quoted ibid.

"and that was . . .": John Huston, quoted ibid.

"abusing witnesses . . .": Arthur Krock, "The Critics of Congress," *New York Times*, October 29, 1947.

"a group . . ." and "legislate the . . .": "Congress Urged to End Un-American Committee," *Washington Post*, October 30, 1947.

"intimidate and stifle . . .": Quoted ibid.

"persecution of those . . .": *Los Angeles Times*, October 25, 1947.

"a veritable . . .": Kahn, p. 78.

"a determined . . ." and "liked to write . . .": Lardner, p. 144.

"not pertinent . . .": Thomas, HUAC 1947, p. 330.

"As indicated . . .": Dalton Trumbo, quoted in Kahn, p. 82.

"If you conduct yourself . . .": Thomas, HUAC 1947, p. 330.

"I shall ask . . .": Stripling, HUAC 1947, p. 331.

"Very many questions . . .": Dalton Trumbo, HUAC 1947, p. 331.

"should answer . . .": Thomas, HUAC 1947, p. 331.

"20 scripts . . .": Trumbo, HUAC 1947, p. 331.

"Too many . . .": Thomas, HUAC 1947, p. 332.

"Mr. Stripling . . .": Trumbo, HUAC 1947, p. 332.

"Can't you answer . . .": Thomas, HUAC 1947, p. 332.

"Mr. Chairman . . .": Trumbo, p. 333.

"Somebody in the audience . . .": Kahn, p. 81.

"Excuse . . .": Thomas, HUAC 1947, p. 333.

"the $64 question": Kahn, p. 81.

"Are you now . . .": Stripling, HUAC 1947, p. 333.

"You must have . . .": Trumbo, HUAC 1947, p. 333.

"Yes, we do": John McDowell, HUAC 1947, p. 333.

"I believe I have . . .": Trumbo, HUAC 1947, p. 334.

"Well, you will . . ." and "The witness . . .": Thomas, HUAC 1947, p. 334.

"This is the . . .": Trumbo, HUAC 1947, p. 334.

"Just a . . .": Thomas, HUAC 1947, p. 334.

"Of an American . . .": Trumbo, HUAC 1947, p. 334.

"This is typical . . .": Thomas, HUAC 1947, p. 334.

"nine pages": Stripling, HUAC 1947, p. 334.

"Mr. Trumbo has never. . .": Ibid.

"The evidence . . .": Thomas, HUAC 1947, p. 342.

"I am an American . . .": Albert Maltz, HUAC 1947, p. 364.

"writers . . . must be . . .": Albert Maltz, quoted in Michael Mills, "The Tragedy of Albert Maltz," *Moderntimes* (blog), www. moderntimes.com/maltz/, accessed December 26, 2016.

"If it requires . . .": Maltz, HUAC 1947, p. 365.

"I would rather die . . .": Ibid., pp. 365–66.

"I have answered . . .": Ibid., p. 366.

"Now either . . .": Alvah Bessie, HUAC 1947, p. 384.

"to the throttling . . .": Ibid., p. 385.

"I don't think . . .": Thomas, HUAC 1947, p. 393.

"I wouldn't . . .": McDowell, HUAC 1947, p. 403.

"a serious question . . ." and "practicing intimidation": Samuel Ornitz, HUAC 1947, pp. 403–4.

"The witness is . . .": Thomas, HUAC 1947, p. 405.

"I was born . . .": Herbert Biberman, HUAC 1947, p. 412.

"another case . . .": Thomas, HUAC 1947, p. 413.

"Mr. Chairman, I would be . . .": Biberman, HUAC 1947, p. 414.

"Take him . . .": Thomas, HUAC 1947, p. 414.

"attacked anti-Semitism . . .": Kahn, p. 105.

"the first to use . . .": Dmytryk, p. 32.

"typical of the other . . .": Thomas, HUAC 1947, p. 460.

"that the producers . . .": Edward Dmytryk, quoted in Kahn, p. 111.

"caused the Chairman . . .": Kahn, p. 105.

"This may not . . .": Thomas, HUAC 1947, p. 466.

"Today this committee . . .": Adrian Scott, quoted in Kahn, p. 107.

"at the hearing room . . .": Kahn, p. 113.

"subpoena from Mr. Thomas . . .": Ring Lardner Jr., "My Life on the Blacklist," *Saturday Evening Post*, October 14, 1961, p. 39.

"I want to be cooperative . . .": Ring Lardner Jr., HUAC 1947, p. 480.

"Now, Mr. Lardner . . .": Thomas, HUAC 1947, p. 480.

"Leave the witness . . .": Ibid., p. 482.

"I think I am . . .": Lardner, HUAC 1947, p. 482.

"Sergeant, take . . .": Thomas, HUAC 1947, p. 482.

"Mr. Chairman . . .": Lester Cole, HUAC 1947, p. 486.

"commies that you're . . .": Louis B. Mayer, quoted in Cole, p. 272.

"You're a very generous man . . .": Quoted in Cole, p. 272.

"My turn came . . .": Cole, p. 284.

"You will not ask . . .": Thomas, HUAC 1947, p. 487.

"The little fat man . . .": Cole, p. 284.

"It is a very simple . . .": Thomas, HUAC 1947, p. 487.

"It isn't necessarily . . .": Cole, HUAC 1947, p. 487.

"Are you able . . .": Thomas, HUAC 1947, p. 487.

"I am not able . . .": Cole, HUAC 1947, p. 487.

"First, we want": Thomas, HUAC 1947, p. 487.

"It was just . . .": Kahn, p. 121.

"Are you now . . .": Stripling, HUAC 1947, p. 494.

"I am a guest . . .": Bertolt Brecht, HUAC 1947, p. 494.

"Mr. Brecht, is it true . . .": Stripling, HUAC 1947, p. 494.

"I have written . . .": Brecht, HUAC 1947, p. 494.

"We are not interested . . .": Thomas, HUAC 1947, p. 494.

"from an examination . . .": Stripling, HUAC 1947, p. 494.

"pro-Communist or . . .": Ibid., p. 496.

"literature has the right. . .": Brecht, HUAC 1947, p. 496.

"Have you ever made . . .": Stripling, HUAC 1947, p. 502.

"No, no, no . . .": Brecht, HUAC 1947, p. 502.

"Being called before . . .": Bertolt Brecht, quoted in Kahn, p. 126.

"You are a good . . .": Thomas, HUAC 1947, p. 504.

"Brecht grieved . . .": Cole, p. 285.

"Mr. Russell, can you . . .": Stripling, HUAC 1947, p. 511.

"that Soviet spies . . .": "House Quiz Presses New Leads in Red Atomic
    Bomb Conspiracy," *Brooklyn Daily Eagle*, October 31, 1947, p. 1.

"the Hollywood personalities . . .": Ibid.

"The hearings today . . .": Thomas, HUAC 1947, p. 522.

"The industry should . . .": Ibid.

CHAPTER 4

"extensive campaign . . ." and "to confuse . . .": J. Parnell Thomas, quoted in Kahn, p. 156.

"Should a committee . . .": Herman P. Eberharter, quoted ibid., p. 158.

"We can support . . .": Ibid., pp. 158–59.

"arrogant": John McDowell, quoted in Kahn, p. 167.

"dispense with . . .": Quoted in "Film Industry to Ban Known Communists," *New York Times*, November 22, 1947.

"The remaining . . .": Jay Walz, "Ten Film Men Cited for Contempt in Overwhelming Votes by House," *New York Times*, November 25, 1947.

"The Constitution was . . .": Thomas, quoted ibid.

"because our investigation . . .": Ibid.

"The Hollywood hearings . . .": Helen Gahagan Douglas, quoted in Kahn, 171.

"the authority of . . .": Tom C. Clark, quoted in Walz, "Ten Film Men Cited."

"every free institution . . .": Quoted in Trumbo, p. 46.

"had privately . . .": Cole, p. 278.

"a national policy . . .": "Asks Rule on Jobs for Communists," *New York Times*, November 20, 1947.

"must . . . take positive steps . . .": Johnston, quoted ibid.

"discharge or suspend . . .": Johnston, quoted in "Movies to Oust Ten Cited for Contempt of Congress," *New York Times*, November 26, 1947.

"suspended": Bosley Crowther, "A Business Matter," *New York Times*, December 7, 1947.

"If the motion picture . . .": Eric Johnston, quoted in "Asks Rule on Jobs for Communists."

"It should be realized . . .": Crowther, "A Business Matter," *New York Times*, December 7, 1947.

"My recent trip . . .": Humphrey Bogart, press release, December 3[, 1947], Huston Collection, f1584, Margaret Herrick Library, Academy of Motion Picture Arts and Sciences, Beverly Hills, CA.

"that there were only . . .": Hedda Hopper, "Looking at Hollywood," *Los Angeles Times*, September 3, 1947.

"up to ridicule . . .": Ibid.

"at a time . . .": Ibid.

"My blood boiled . . .": Florence George Crosby, letter to Hedda Hopper, November 7, 1947, Hedda Hopper Collection, f1010, Margaret Herrick Library, Academy of Motion Picture Arts and Sciences, Beverly Hills, CA.

"ignoring the feeling . . .": Irene Walker, letter to Hedda Hopper, February 26, 1948, Hedda Hopper Collection, f775, Margaret Herrick Library Academy of Motion Picture Arts and Sciences, Beverly Hills, CA.

"This is applicable . . .": Ibid.

"was in the process . . .": Charles Houston, quoted in "Trumbo Convicted of Congress Contempt; Film Writer Faces Jail in Communist Case," *New York Times*, May 6, 1948.

"in the early morning . . .": Cole, p. 296.

"In a few weeks . . .": Dmytryk, p. 94.

"to disguise . . .": Cole, p. 297.

"The informant . . .": FBI file on Lester Cole, n.d., L.A. 46-1844.

"If they couldn't prosecute . . .": Cole, p. 297.

"SUGGEST BUREAU DETERMINE . . .": FBI file on Lester Cole, September 28, 1949, 46-16420-5.

"was in England . . .": FBI file on Lester Cole, "Current Activities of the Hollywood Ten," n.d., LA 100-15732, p. 42.

"has been active . . .": Ibid., p. 43.

"The History of Anti-Semitism . . .": Ibid., p. 44.

"attended a meeting . . .": Ibid., p. 45.

"writing . . ." and "raising . . .": Ibid., p. 46.

"appeared on the radio . . ." and "attacking . . .": Ibid.

"devotion to Americanism . . .": John Howard Lawson, FBI file on Lester Cole, n.d., LA 100-15732, p. 47.

"dogmatic . . .": Leon Yankwich, quoted in Gladwin Hill, "Johnston Assailed by Film Case Judge," *New York Times*, December 21, 1948.

"$1,350-a-week . . .": Ibid.

"ordered payment . . .": Ibid.

"the position that Congress . . .": "Contempt Appeal Lost by 2 Film Men," *New York Times*, June 14, 1949.

"We hold that . . .": Quoted ibid.

"It is fully established . . .": Ibid.

"President Truman . . .": Cole, p. 310.

"names of outsiders . . .": Alexander Holtzoff, quoted in C. P. Trussell, "Thomas Gets 6 to 18 Months, Fined $10,000 in Pay Fraud," *New York Times*, December 10, 1949.

"to her own . . .": Ibid.

"true Americanism": Ibid.

"was upheld . . .": Lewis Wood, "Film Writers Lose Contempt Appeal," *New York Times*, April 11, 1950.

"had sold . . .": Cole, p. 310.

"spoke of how . . .": Ibid., p. 313.

"'You couldn't . . . Amendment?' . . .": Ibid.

"had hit a solid . . .": Dmytryk, p. 96.

"I borrowed . . .": Ibid., p. 111.

"We are financially . . .": Albert Maltz, quoted in Ceplair and Englund, p. 354.

"only six months . . .": Dmytryk, p. 118.

"fitted with leg irons . . .": Dmytryk, p. 126.

"His job . . .": Cole, p. 319.

"I see just like . . .": Quoted in Cole, p. 320.

"A few of the writers . . .": Lardner, "My Life on the Blacklist," p. 38.

"I was not a communist . . .": Dmytryk, p. 146.

"I dearly wished . . .": Ibid., p. 150.

"support could be made . . .": Ibid., p. 151.

"splashed all over . . .": Ibid.

"This blacklisted status . . .": Lardner, "My Life on the Blacklist,"
    p. 38.

"To force a man . . .": Larry Parks, quoted in "Larry Parks," Spartacus
    Educational, http://spartacus-educational.com/USAparks.htm,
    accessed January 1, 2017.

"The Ten stoutly . . .": Judge Robert W. Kenny to Albert Maltz, letter,
    March 22, 1973, Lester Cole Papers.

"I am most willing . . .": Lillian Hellman to Honorable John S.
    Wood, letter, May 19, 1952, in Christine Blackerby, "Pleading
    the Fifth: Lillian Hellman and the HUAC Investigation of
    Hollywood," *Social Education* 80, no 6 (2016): 316–20,
    https://www.socialstudies.org/publications/socialeducation/
    november-december2016/pleading-fifth-lillian-hellman-and-huac-
    investigation-of-hollywood, accessed January 1, 2017.

"if your Committee . . .": Ibid.

"with Louis Pollack . . .": Ceplair and Englund, p. 388.

"Eighteenth Century-Fox": Samuel "Zero" Mostel, *Investigation of
    Communist Activities, New York Area—Part VIII (Entertainment)*,
    p. 2491.

"refuse either to . . .": Dalton Trumbo, dialogue in *Trumbo*, directed
    by Peter Askin, 2007; DVD (Magnolia Home Entertainment,
    2009), at 75:10.

"In fact . . .": Lardner, "My Life on the Blacklist," p. 43.

"Trumbo tied . . .": James Lardner, "The Dalton Trumbo I Knew,"
    New Republic, February 24, 2016, https://newrepublic.com/
    article/130451/dalton-trumbo-knew, accessed September 24, 2016.

CHAPTER 5

"a kind of central . . .": Ceplair and Englund, p. 419.

"used at least . . .": Chris Trumbo, quoted in Jack Mathews, "Children of the Blacklist: Growing Up During Hollywood's Most Shameful Era," *Los Angeles Times Magazine*, October 15, 1989, p. 14.

"the head of . . .": Mathews, "Children of the Blacklist," p. 14.

"was an idealist . . .": Jeffrey Lawson, quoted ibid., p. 16.

"was thrown out . . ." and "[had] been involved . . .": Alvah Bessie, quoted in Eileen Keerdoja, "Update," *Newsweek*, January 24, 1977, p. 10.

"went from . . .": Lester Cole, quoted ibid.

"To use my own . . .": Cole, p. 400.

"In April 1977 . . .": Lester Cole, "'Hollywood 10': A Survivor's Update," letter to the editor, *New York Times*, April 7, 1978.

"There may possibly be . . .": Quoted in Lardner, "My Life on the Blacklist," p. 42.

"The people for whom . . .": Lardner, "My Life on the Blacklist," p. 42.

"The First Amendment prohibits . . .": Vaughn, p. 285.

INDEX

165

PICTURE CREDITS

Birmingham Sunday

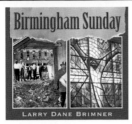

Orbis Pictus Award Honor Book
A *Kirkus Reviews* Best Children's Book
Jane Addams Honor Book for Older Children
★ *Kirkus Reviews*, STARRED REVIEW
★ *Library Media Connection*, STARRED REVIEW
★ *School Library Journal*, STARRED REVIEW

Black & White: The Confrontation between Reverend Fred L. Shuttlesworth and Eugene "Bull" Connor

Sibert Honor Book
Carter G. Woodson Book Award
ALSC Notable Children's Book
Norman A. Sugarman Children's Biography Honor Award
Booklist Top 10 Black History Book for Youth
Notable Books for a Global Society Book Award
A Chicago Public Library Best of the Best Book
A *Kirkus Reviews* Best Children's Book
★ *Booklist*, STARRED REVIEW
★ *Kirkus Reviews*, STARRED REVIEW

Twelve Days in May: Freedom Ride 1961

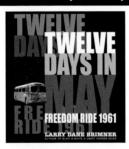

Sibert Medal Winner
Booklist Editors' Choice
A Chicago Public Library Best of the Best Book
★ *Booklist*, STARRED REVIEW
★ *School Library Journal*, STARRED REVIEW

We Are One: The Story of Bayard Rustin

Jane Addams Book Award for Older Children
Norman A. Sugarman Children's Biography Award
New York Public Library Books for the Teen Age
★ *School Library Connection*, STARRED REVIEW
★ *School Library Journal*, STARRED REVIEW